Retouching from start to finish

by Veronica Cass,
Craftsman Photographer

Published by TR Book Publishers, 1312 Lincoln Boulevard,
Santa Monica, California 90406

Preface

This book is dedicated to Fine Arts of Photography and to the competent artists who have helped to make it a progressive field.

Fine Arts of Photography . . . the difference between amateur and professional. Through "professionalism," this field has developed.

This three part book, covering the receptionist and make up, negative retouching and print retouching and restoration, serves as a textbook to this fascinating art. Through reading this book, it is my hope that you will be helped to overcome the common headaches of studios and labs.

INTRODUCTION

Retouching . . . the neglected art

The idea of retouching began with a guild type of training. Ideas and teaching methods were passed on for years without much change . . . more or less a "hand-me-down" art. Slowly, a few schools began teaching it.

When I first started retouching, I quit three times out of frustration. I always wanted to know the whys and how to's. I thought there should be something different and more applicable to today's negatives.

When I decided to begin teaching retouching, I hesitated because I did things differently. I knew my method was correct because the end results were excellent. A friend recommended that I teach retouching two ways — my way and the way others do.

I've been successful using my method, which is in reality a combination of personal ideas and experiences incorporated with that of many great retouchers. I tell students at my school, Veronica Cass School of Retouching, Hudson, Florida, "I can teach you all that I have learned and a few of my ideas. When you get it all together, then do your own thing. Use the method(s) most suited to you."

I always look for short cuts to help reduce the work without quality loss, which is especially important during the rush season when speed and efficiency are anecessity.

Being on the National Retouchers Committee of the Professional Photographers of America and serving as a judge in this field has given me the opportunity to see the work of several excellent retouchers.

When I see work that is natural and complementary to the subject, I seek out the retoucher to find out the methods that were used.

Many great people in the photographic field started as retouchers and have worked persistently to make improvements. They recognize what can be done and have had the desire to help others improve their photography.

My primary goal in this book is to show improvements that can be made in front of the camera, on the negative and on the print, hopefully educating the aspiring photographer and retoucher.

Dedication

Dedicated to my family and to the many wonderful friends who have helped make this dream come true through their never-ending encouragement.

TABLE OF CONTENTS

CHAPTER ONE

Hiring a good receptionist

We often hear the comment, "A receptionist can make or break a photographer." True! A good receptionist is the coordinator for the photographer, the customer and the retoucher. Therefore, it is important to look for specific qualities in the selection of a receptionist.

Personal appearance should be a key consideration. The receptionist should have a neat appearance and use good sense in dress. Jeans and trendy shirts are not well-suited for a professional climate.

It's good business sense to have a person with a pleasing personality, who likes people and has an interest in photography. Although photographic background is not a necessity, some interest in photography would be helpful in understanding specific wants and needs.

A receptionist should possess an artistic sense and have an understanding of color coordination (e.g. dress, jewelry) to assist customers.

Once the receptionist is found and hired, provide proper training. Don't expect this employee to read minds, and don't expect to turn the business over to the receptionist in just a few weeks and expect miracles. Just as you, the employer, have experienced training, so too will the receptionist need it. The receptionist should understand the photographer's moods, be helpful to the customer, and, above all, should know what can and cannot be done on a negative or print.

Begin with the telephone basics. Explain how the phone is to be answered. Keep a pad and pencil beside the phone, permitting the receptionist to write the caller's name and outline the message. If the caller is a current customer, their worksheet or file should be pulled. People calling for advice should be dealing with someone who knows what they're talking about. Teach the receptionist what can and cannot be done in color, how color affects the photograph and about costly corrections.

A customer calling for an appointment will usually inquire about the service's cost. This information should be provided honestly — the camera charge, sitting cost, etc. The receptionist should ask the customer the use of the portrait and then suggest clothing and makeup ideas.

This interest shows concern about producing a good photograph. A studio or business, where a complete lack of interest is shown by the employees, provides an uncomfortable feeling for the client. By making a few subtle suggestions, a person's confidence can be gained.

Clothing should not be overly bright, too abstract in print or too bulky for a memorable photograph. Simplicity is the *key* for all subjects.

Dark tones or those on the warmer side such as brown, navy or maroon are appropriate, as these colors will not distract from the individual's face. If your business is located in a temperate area, lighter clothing colors will most likely dominate. Here, too, they should not be distracting. Photographers located in warm areas where customers often have tans should accent the color.

A new receptionist should have a simple check list to use as a guideline.

1. Greet the customer in a genuine, pleasant manner.

2. Be unobtrusively observant of the customer. Check for wrinkled clothing or messy hair and, most of all, disturbing or unsightly bright or dark blemishes. (Complete instruction on pre-photo attention is described later in this chapter.)

3. Keep notes on decisions made at the time proofs (previews) are returned. If the customer wants a mole removed, this should be noted in the file to avoid any future problem. Use a professional note tablet or

form to explain to client any problems which may occur or note if the client is making an impossible request.

To avoid any future problems, the receptionist must keep good notes both in the files and on each customer's worksheet. Many receptionists handling this important information are inadequately trained in marking proofs (previews).

Training a receptionist properly is part of a long-term investment in business. Doing it right from the beginning can save both time and money and can also prevent future problems.

CHAPTER TWO

Makeup in front of the camera: the legal way for photographers

Laws differ throughout the United States in the area of cosmetology. Application of makeup in front of the camera must comply to these specifications. The photographer or receptionist cannot touch the customer's face.

A professional studio should be equipped with makeup to permit a polished presentation. No matter how well done the lighting, background and pose, the customer with a skin problem or dark circles under the eyes will consider these imperfections on the previews. Providing basic makeup is a worthwhile preliminary step.

There are several things a receptionist can do without a cosmetologist's license, correctly touching up problem areas before the camera in a quick, safe, efficient manner. Makeup should be applied as needed, explaining to the customer that the previews will appear better and art work will be reduced. Natural color should be left natural. Only the weak areas should be covered or enhanced. The negative may still have to be retouched, but the customer will be happier to see a more flattering proof.

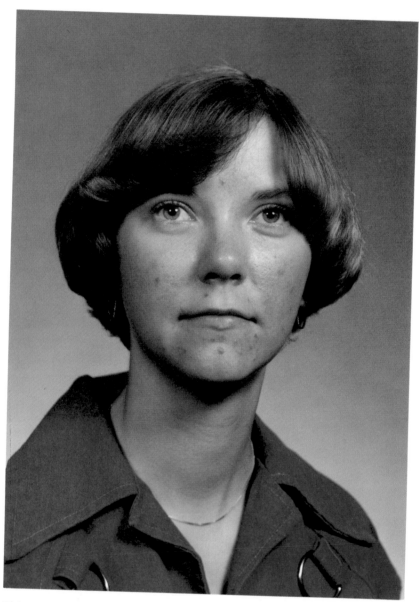

Girl with blemishes in front of camera before proper makeup.

Same girl after makeup has been properly applied.

Supplies

The following items will take care of all makeup problems and needs and should always be kept in stock. All makeup should be placed by the camera or reception desk, not accessible to public use, and should be hypo-allergenic.

Cotton balls
Tissues
Q-tips
Face powder (colorless)
Liquid base makeup in three basic
  shades for normal skin
Makeup (cover-up) stick in two
  shades

Brown eyebrow pencil
Dry-cake powder blush in a
  natural shade
Lipstick in a natural shade
Hair spray
Clean combs
Lip gloss

Makeup is used to:
1. Cover blemishes, scars, bites, and blue beards
2. Enchance the color of cheeks and lips
3. Add density to the eyebrows
4. Tone down hot spots
Each problem area will be discussed separately.

Eye makeup

All eye makeup should be applied by the customer under the direction of the receptionist. If the eyebrows are too light, a soft brown makeup pencil should be used to apply color ONLY to the brow hairs. Brows can be applied to the customer by the receptionist. Turn the pencil vertically and side-ways to coat the hairs — the flesh is not to be touched. A brown eyebrow stick is all that is needed as blonde or light brown haired people ususaly need the extra coloring. The aim is to add density to show more in the photograph. The rest of the eye makeup should be applied by the customer to avoid possible legal problems.

Be aware of white or luminescent eye shadows — these photograph ghastly and ghostly. Since they accent all of the lines, they may make older women look older. Discreetly warn the customer about this, or, better yet, show them samples of how these photograph.

Eye lash accent should always be regarded as an improvement. The customer should apply a minimal amount of mascara. If they like eyeliner, have them apply it sparingly. Caution in the application of color under the eyes must be taken. This often causes a retouching problem. If used, it should be a neutral shade. This should be noted by the receptionist for the retoucher.

To add color to brow, turn medium brown soft pencil sideways, stroking just the hairs of the brow, giving a natural darkening.

Hair

When the customer first arrives for a sitting, hair will most likely be out of order (disheveled). Show the customer to the dressing room where hair can be styled in the way it will appear on the photograph. Consider placing a sign in the dressing room stating "The way you look now is the way you'll photograph." Only minor corrections can be made in natural color.

Always keep freshly cleaned combs on hand for customers who have forgotten theirs. Combs can be purchased inexpensively from novelty companies. If they continue having problems keeping hair in place during the sitting, the receptionist should ask for permission to fix loose strands. When hair is unmanageable, too thin to hold shape or freshly washed or cut, hair spray should be used.

Apply spray in a manner that will not offend the customer. Spray over their head or on your hands. Glide hands over the head slightly, touching the hair. This will make fly-away hairs lay down. Untended, these hairs will pick up the highlights and therefore cost dollars and hours to spot them out. Another way is to spray a facial tissue and wipe it over the hair.

If the customer has long and fine hair, carefully brush it forward and arrange around the shoulders. This will make the hair look heavier. Beautiful hair is a woman's "crowning glory." The receptionist can enhance the beauty of female customers with care and thought.

The same consideration should be shown for men. Fly-away hairs should be smoothed down. Watch out for the customer who, after seeing the proof, decides her child would look better with a haircut. This should have been handled before the photography was done. Make sure to charge at least as much as a barber would for this retouching job. The same is also true for men who want their mustaches removed after the fact.

When a customer requests that impossible hair corrections be made, explain that only minor hair retouching is done. Large hair corrections must be done by an artist. Give the customer an estimate of the cost. Art corrections generally run at a set price per hour, depending upon location.

When using hairspray to control stray hairs, apply spray above subject's head.

Left: Another way of controlling stray strands is to spray hand and then glide it over the subject's hair, being careful not to alter hair style.

Right: When applying hairspray by hand, gently glide hand over hair, being careful not to press down on hair style.

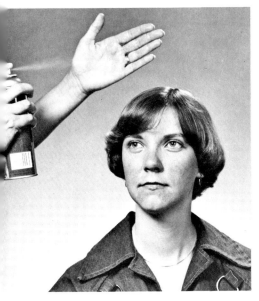

Face

Carefully study the customer's face. Are there any marks that they most likely will not want to appear on the print? These will be such flaws as:

Blemishes	Scars	Cuts
Cold Sores	Bruises	Prominent Freckles
Moles	Bites	Dark Circles under the Eyes

Young people often have blemish problems, of which they are sensitive. They usually prefer having a little makeup applied correctly so their proofs will not contain these blemishes.

When suggesting use of makeup to cover the blemishes, make sure the customer understands it is a pure, non-allergenic makeup. Show them how to apply the makeup with Q-tips; or if they prefer, have the receptionist apply it. Be careful, the receptionist's hands must never touch the customer's face.

Also, proofs should not look like mass production — "Let natural color be natural." Basic skin should show, only the blemish or blemishes should be covered. Use a color slightly darker than the skin tone to avoid trouble. Makeup that is too light may create another print problem in spotting. A Q-tip should be used to apply a small amount of either the liquid or stick makeup on the blemish only. Do not overlap. Turn the tip around, using the other end to blend the makeup or wipe off any excess. Use caution working with a customer with a really bad complexion. After covering a few spots, throw the Q-tips away and use a fresh one.

Upper left: To cover blemishes, apply non-allergenic makeup with Q-tip.

Upper right: When covering blemishes, remember that only the blemish area should be covered - basic skin should show.

Lower left: Wipe off excess makeup with opposite side of Q-tip, remembering not to overlap and allowing the natural skin tone to remain.

Lower right: Sometimes fatigue lines and/or circles under the eyes need toning down. Add makeup only to area in need of correction.

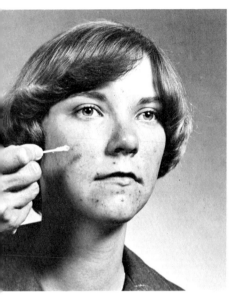

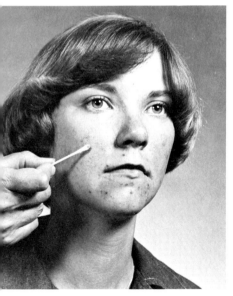

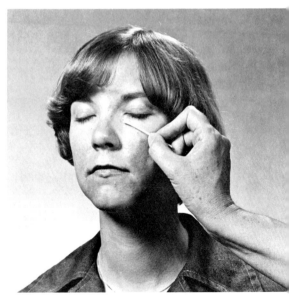

Freckles

Freckles that are natural to a customer's face should not be removed. There are times, however, when the freckles are very bright and are gathered in clumps. To help tone these down, apply a thin layer of liquid base makeup in a shade similar to the natural coloring. Be careful not to apply it too thickly or in a shade that's too light or dark — creating print problems and making the customer look unnatural. Should the customer want all the freckles removed on the negative, state that the charge for this will be considerably higher as it requires an art correction. This will generally encourage the customer to change his or her mind. Handle this particular problem at the time of proof presentation.

Oily skin

Oily skin or too much glossy makeup causes a shine that shows up in photographs, appearing on the negative as overly bright and shiny areas. This will mean a lot of blending for the retoucher. A large white spot on the forehead will be caused by light reflecting. There will be little hot spots on all the raised blemishes on a poor complexion. After these are retouched, they will look as though the retoucher did a poor job.

To tone down oily skin, apply a small amount of neutral colored powder on the face with a cotton ball. Fluff off excess with same cotton ball on the opposite side. Do not rub the face while doing this or it could cause red to appear on some people's complexions.

Moles — facial marks

If the customer has an obvious mole or beauty mark (as it is sometimes called), ask whether or not it is to appear on the photograph. If the response is negative, cover it as a blemish. It's much easier to correct it at this point than for the retoucher to remove it later. Most often, though, characteristic marks such as these are left to the discretion of the photographer, making the picture appear more natural.

Perhaps the customer doesn't have blemish or mole problems but is definitely lacking color. If they are too pale, suggest that cheek color (a brownish-red blush) will enhance natural skin tone. Apply blush to the cheek bone area, an inch below the eye to about a half inch from the nose with a fresh cotton ball.

To tone down oily skin, apply a small amount of neutral colored powder with a cotton ball.

When adding color to lips, use a natural color and apply with Q-tip, adding color mainly to the bottom lip.

For dry lips, apply lip gloss in the middle of the bottom lip only.

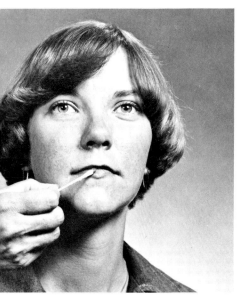

If the customer's lips lack color or have little definition, add some color with a flesh or brownish-red lipstick. For lips that are too dry, apply a little lip gloss in the middle of the bottom lip only. Too much would be distracting. Apply lipstick as an outline and then blend in.

Beards

Some men have heavy beards, the kind that creates the "5 o'clock shadow" problem. These blue beards show up noticeably on the print. This can be corrected before shooting by applying a very thin layer of liquid makeup with the finger tips over the "bluish" area. Cotton or tissue will stick to the beard and should therefore not be used. Show the customer how this is to be done or get permission to apply it, being sure makeup is blended in well.

Glasses

There is definite lack of understanding with respect to glasses, artistically speaking. Both photographers and customer need to be educated on glasses. If a person walks in wearing glasses and poses with them on, this customer needs them. The glasses are part of that person. Therefore, artistically speaking, all the shadows should not be removed. The photograph will not look natural. Observe the person wearing the glasses, noting the shadows. Avoid any problems by having the receptionist explain that shadows should only be toned down, not completely removed.

If the glass lenses are very thick, request that the customer ask their optometrist for an empty pair of frames for the photograph. This can save countless problems, such as refraction of flesh, glares on glasses, and enlarging or diminishing the eyes, and still look quite natural. (Of course this can only be requested if glass thickness is known of prior to the visit.)

CHAPTER THREE

Sales

Preparing the subject in front of the camera is important to good sales; but equally as valuable a sales step is the presentation of the previews, proofs or originals. Photographs should be presented with finesse, giving value to each individual, making the customer feel important.

Presentation of proofs:

How this is done is definitely important to sales.

1. Look at the proofs with the customer(s).
2. Show proofs in presentation folders.
3. Make suggestions.
4. Get the second deposit.

Take time to look at the proofs with the customers. Place the proofs or previews in matts, folders, or booklets to protect the photos. This is especially important for originals. A black box with gold stretch band can be used to provide an attractive display for the customer. As you talk with the customer, made suggestions. Point out which are the

When presenting proofs, a black box with gold stretch band provides an attractive display for customer approval.

more flattering poses or which have the best composition. Ask for the second deposit on the order and establish a date when the proofs must be returned.

When the customer returns the proofs:

1. No matter what, be pleased with their choice.
2. Check proof to see if any special corrections are needed. Do this in front of the customer.
3. Mark proof on the area in need of correction, using an inexpensive wax pencil that can be easily wiped off later.
4. Only after the order has been taken:
   a. suggest selling previews in matts
   b. depending on the size of order, price accordingly
5. Special color corrections:
   a. only certain corrections can be made in color
   b. unusual correction are costly
   c. instruct customer that glasses leave natural shadows
   d. colors in clothing and background can be enhanced

Regardless of personal opinion, be pleased with the customer's choice. Listen to customer's comments. They may notice things about themselves in the photographs which have been overlooked, such as an eyebrow out of place or an unnatural shadow. Note any corrections to be made while reviewing proofs with the customer.

Marking the proof at this time assures good communication. Many times the sales department or receptionist fail to communicate the customer's message to the retoucher or art department. A marked proof can prevent this from happening, allowing no misunderstanding. Retouchers often complain about weird requests with no explanations. These can cause both the retoucher and the customer problems.

Corrections should be marked on the proof with an inexpensive wax pencil, a BWS marking pen or even a black Lumocolor pencil. This can be easily cleaned off the preview after but shows the customer that the preview is being marked so that the retoucher or artist will notice it. When the order is completed, these marks can be wiped off with facial tissue, keeping the proofs saleable. BWS and Lumo markers need another cleaning method.

The receptionist should understand what the retoucher can do and what the artist can do, plus have an understanding of how much time some of these corrections can take. A minor correction would be absorbed under normal retouching costs, but a large correction will be billed at an hourly charge, obviously costing more.

Note any needed corrections while reviewing proofs with customer, assuring good communication.

Tell the customer that only certain corrections can be made in color. Unusual corrections are costly, and unless it is a mistake of the photographer, the customer will have to absorb these costs. For example, if strap marks on a draped customer hasn't been toned down in front of the camera, it will be difficult to remove them on the negative or print.

Clothing and background can be enhanced or slightly changed with dyes. This is referring to the light areas. Changes in the darker areas are more costly, necessitating correction by a colorist using heavy oils, acrylics or airbrush.

If the customer makes an unusual request, have them sign the work sheet. This will serve as protection for the photographer.

An added benefit for any studio in the sales and management areas would be the book, "A Lifetime of Successful Portrait Studio Management and Sales Techniques" by Edith Garrett, available from her in Columbus, Georgia. This outlined and well-indexed handbook has some great ideas and information.

Account# _____

Studio or Lab _____

I have done as much retouching as possible on this negative, and hope it will be satisfactory.

Problem: _____

_____

_____

_____

Retoucher _____

To insure proper communication between studio and lab and retoucher, a simple note form should always be used, allowing for little misunderstanding.

Photo courtesy of James Bright Backgrounds

22

CHAPTER FOUR

Backgrounds

Indoors

An important part of portrait photography is the background. It has an extreme influence on color in retouching as well as print corrections. Today there are, unfortunately, too many poorly selected background colors, creating problems for the retoucher and artist.

Bright blues in the background cause color to bounce, giving every shadow on the subject a hidden blue cast. When the retoucher removes the density from under the eyes, moles or the necklines, the blue may remain, as many do not see it on the negative. Those retouchers who don't get a proof with the negative will really have problems.

What color background should be used? I recommend selecting a color that will complement the skin tone and not cause reflections.

Following is a diagram and suggested background for photographers who want to paint their own background. The color blends with the Vericolor negative because it doesn't print too warmly.

Supplies Required:

Canvas or wall board
Water Base paint or
    acrylics
Pails or large pans

Wide point brush, a large sponge,
    or a mop
You can even use spray cans or
    an air brush

23

Recommended Color Combinations

Burnt Umber (Brown)
  (or something similar)
Payne's Gray (which has a blue
  tint to it)

Titanium White (a pure white)
Moss Green or Hooker's Green as
  an accent (a natural earthy
  green)

Acrylics are very easy to blend and can be thinned with water for easier application and for areas needing lightening or darkening.

If brown is the desired color, make the brown background first. Mix a small portion (now, this depends on the size being painted) of the brown and white, this will make a beautiful tan.

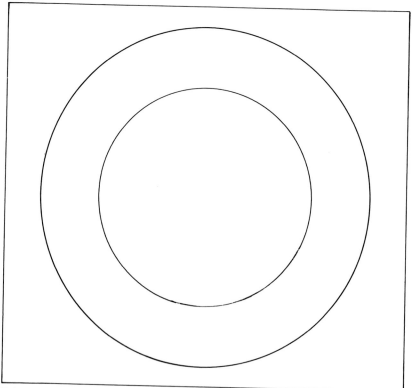

Paint outer circle brown — work to inner circle and gradually pick up the tan. Blend with brown and tan.

For a color accent, take a little Payne's Gray, thinned with water, and put a little over the brown. This color has a subtle amount of blue in it, called a wash.

A touch of the green can also be added. Use a Moss Green or Hooker's Green, nothing too bright. With lights on, the reddish-brown comes through the added colors, enough to complement the skin tones or any clothing. There is red in the Burnt Umber, a suggestion of blue in Payne's Gray, and in the green there is a small amount of yellow. All are so muted and blended that they can only complement and not distract.

Using the same color combination, switch the main color to Payne's Gray. Lightly add white for blending and then use Burnt Umber for the accent color.

Photo courtesy of James Bright Backgrounds

Take a brush (or sponge) and just lightly add an accent color here and there. You should be able to see the brown come through the Payne's Gray.

If Moss Green is the base, more of the accent color (Burnt Umber) may be necessary and just a little Payne's Gray. Do not allow the green to dominate.

Always keep in mind, the subject of the photograph is most important. Therefore, the background should not be too bright. Rather, it should be darker so as not to compete for attention.

If a background is cool and warm, (which is the combination of the Payne's Gray and Burnt Umber) it will most likely print cool when needed and warm when the influence is there.

Painting a background can be a fun project. To do this correctly, it is best for the photographer to set up the camera and make a test. Paint a small area first and then look at it through the camera. Try to get

Photo courtesy of James Bright Backgrounds

Start with the Burnt Umber first; and as you work to the clouded area you want (this should be measured for seating area) and with the same brush, gradually pick up small amounts of tan. Make sure your tan does not get too light — this would be distracting.

someone to sit and pose as a customer would; this will help insure accuracy in judging the clouded area and allow for a better idea for blending and colors.

Turn the lights on the background as would be necessary for a portrait or for a group — check out the background by taking a color Polaroid of it. This should show how it will look in a portrait setting.

Projected backgrounds

Projected backgrounds often add to photographs but may be deceiving and create some problems. These project color on the subject or may cause the color to bounce. Backgrounds often cast unwanted shadows on the subject which the photographer will want corrected. This is a difficult task.

These backgrounds are generally used with 120 negatives, making the head size rather small, and making the retouching difficult, even for an expert. The solution — study the proof. One has to be able to see the unwanted color to retouch it. Dyes are excellent for this task. See section on applying dyes, Chapter 12.

There is much less retouching needed when the original photography is expertly done, using correct filters. Problems arise when harshness appears on the subject, unwanted colors are all over, and fatigue lines are very dense.

There are seminars given by professional photograph experts, explaining how to avoid most of these problems. Attendance at these seminars should lessen the need for retouching.

Again, the retouching solution is having a proof, which displays the unwanted color. To obtain good retouching, give retouchers the help they need — a proof.

PART 2

Negative retouching

The negative is the heart of the photographic business. Since photography's beginnings, the negative has changed in many ways, always resulting in improvements.

Just as the negative has improved, so too must we as retouchers. The photographer's negatives are entrusted to our skill. It is our work, how and when we retouch, that keeps the work flow moving. Poor retouching leads to excessive spotting on prints, while slow retouching and insufficient placement of importance on the negative will slow production.

Today we work with more color and less black and white negatives. The color negatives are generally Vericolor or a similar type. The negatives are thin, hard, and in general very easy to work with and on.

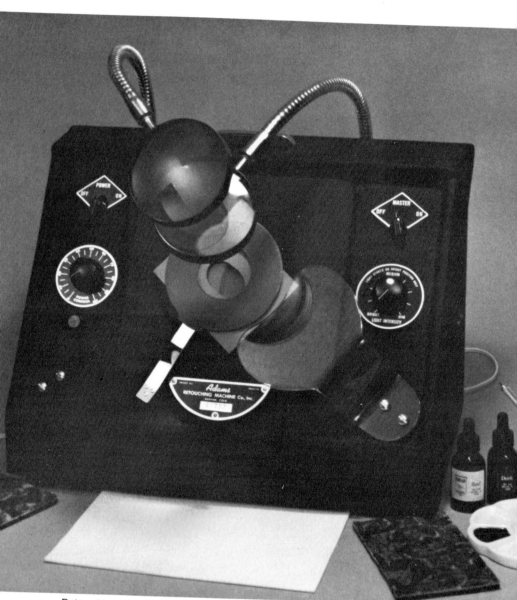

Retouching machine and work area prepared to begin working on negatives.

CHAPTER FIVE

The retouching machine

In negative retouching, I use the Adams Retouching machine. For years I have worked with the Adams people on updating their equipment to fulfill today's retouching needs. The machine case has remained the same, but the inside lighting has been greatly improved. Each machine has one magnifying glass attached, but additional ones are available. I prefer equipping my machines with the second glass because of the small negatives with which we have to work.

How to use a machine

1. First, put on a pair of magnifying glasses. Then turn vibrator to position desired. (It's on the left hand side.)
Note: 10-15 suggested for 120.70mm
    20-25 for b/w 70mm-90mm, 4X5
    45-50 for abrading tool.
2. Turn on power.
3. Set lights to bright. Turn on. (It's on the right.)
4. Turn on master switch.
Since I work every day with the machine, I leave it set and simply press the master switch. There are times when the machine doesn't turn

on, or it appears not to respond. Check your "bright" setting on the light switch. You may find the line on the dial in the wrong position. The light in your machine is fluorescent. If the dial is set to dim, the machine will not turn on.

The machine's negative cage is designed to hold all size negatives. Place your negative inside a mask to avoid getting fingerprints on it. This is helpful when you are working n small negatives as the mask blocks out the excess light.

Turn the handle of the negative cage down and lift the center. Insert the mask (with negative) and turn the handle to upward position. The negative is now in position to begin retouching. (See photos — showing cage position.)

Both handles of the negative cage and the eyes of the subject should be horizontal. This will permit the cage to work for you. While retouching, the left hand will move the negative cage down, working with the contour of the subject's face. When the negative is finished, it will be removed from the starting position. Left-handed retouchers simply move the hand rest to the other side of the machine and work the opposite way.

Keeping updated and using modern equipment is just as important as knowing the new methods and techniques. The retouching machine is

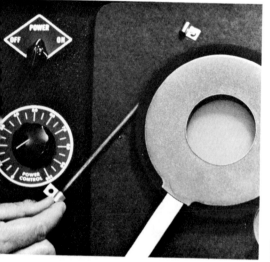

Before turning on machine, remove bar that protects vibrator and place in drawer.

For light intensity, make sure dial is at bright.

The retouching machine can
magnifying glasses, attached
shown.

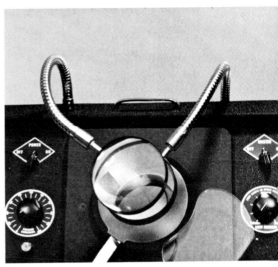

Line up magnifying glasses to suit your
eyes.

The retouching machine is now ready
for work.

Pull handle down and insert mask at
top.

Adjust handle of negative cage to work with contour of face.

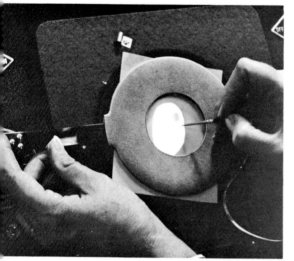

Turn negative and work with contour of face with tip of brush.

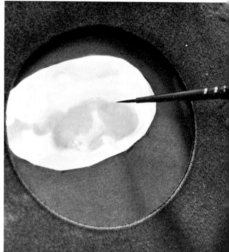

just one of the many important pieces of equipment in the studio or lab which must be maintained to assure a professional touch.

An art department, like the studio and reception area, should receive careful consideration. Both the spotting and retouching areas should be well-planned to suit their purposes. Proper lighting and cleanliness are important.

The retouching area does not need to be large. You can either build a desk with larger drawers or buy one. Place the machine in the middle, about four to six inches from the edge of the desk, directly in front of you. The space under the desk should allow enough room for leg comfort and good circulation.

The desk chair used should have good height and be supportive of the back to avoid tensions. The room should be semi-dark, as bright lights tend to strain one's eyes. If possible, position the desk against a wall where there are no windows. If the room has windows, they should be covered with curtains that are heavy enough to block out light.

The main light to be used while retouching is the one from the retouching machine. A small, high intensity lamp is recommended for studying proofs. Keep that light off when it isn't in use so that it will not become distracting. The best light in the room should be located behind the retoucher. A 40 or 60 watt bulb is all that is necessary.

The other retouching supplies you will need are:

a. White tablet
b. Leads — graphite and colored
c. Sandpaper — 360 superfine
d. Retouching fluid
e. Cotton and/or facial tissue
f. White glove
g. Brushes WN 00 Series 7 — Grambacher 1780000
h. Palette
i. Dyes
j. Plastic water bottle

k. Blue acetate
l. 4X5 envelope for mask and sandpaper
m. Elbow pads
n. Round tooth picks
o. Tool holder — optional
p. Anti-stat
q. Abrading tool
r. Photo Flo
s. Emery polishing paper
t. Opaque

For cleanliness and organization, use a box (or a drawer) to hold sandpapers, mask, bottles of dye and retouching fluid. Keep the envelope holding the sandpaper for sharpening graphite in a vertical position to avoid spillage. Take a half-envelope and fill with cotton to wipe off the graphite after sharpening. Keep it in a convenient position.

Trim sandpaper to envelope size.

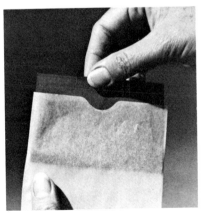

Insert trimmed sandpaper into envelope.

Trim envelope to usable size.

Sandpaper envelope is now ready for use.

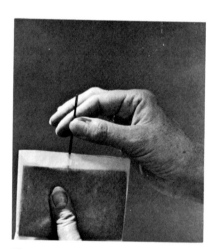

Sharpen graphite in sandpaper envelope.

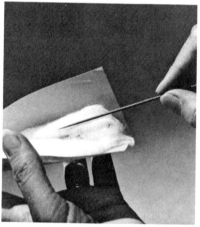

Wipe off excess by utilizing a half envelope filled with cotton.

For elbow comfort, place two 4×6 pieces of rubber-backed carpeting in position on each side of the machine. Let elbows rest in the middle of the carpet. This provides comfort and will prevent the circulation from being cut off.

In front of the machine and between the two elbow pads, place a pad of clean, white paper. The top sheet should be changed daily. This is for doping (applying retouching fluid) negatives and testing dye colors. Each day before beginning to work, clean the area. Use a slightly damp cloth to wipe off dust. Dampness breaks the electrical friction and picks up excess dust, instead of rearranging it. Keep oil or chemical cloths away from the negative retouching area.

Keep the palette clean; don't allow dirt to accumulate. Try to wash the brush at least once a week. Most of all, always protect the negative. Dope it on clean paper and handle it with a mask or glove.

CHAPTER SIX

The retouching brush

A good brush is valuable in controlling work. It is easy to detect when an artist uses an inexpensive brush or a worn out brush by the sloppy retouching or spotting. Select a brush that has a good consistent point and an even flow or spread. I use the Winsor & Newton. I have found that it performs on a consistent basis. The size of the brush determines how it applies dyes and how much it holds.

There are times when the brush will have hairs that will not stay in form. This can happen after a brush is freshly washed or has been left in the wrong position.

To control the brush hairs and get them back in working order, wet the brush and hold it between warm fingers. Do this a few times. The hand's warmth will press the stray hairs back into place.

Caring for the brush

About once a week, I clean my brush. It's a simple method. Stroke brush lightly on a mild bar of soap just a few times; gently squeeze the soap through. Turn tap water on slowly and place brush on hand; let water flow on the brush until soap is out.

Now that the brush is freshly washed, it is like freshly washed hair, out of control. To put it back in control, put the brush into the mouth — saliva is a mild glue and it will hold the hairs in place until needed again. (This is the only time to put the brush into the mouth.)

When the brush is used again, simply saturate and rinse as in the first step when preparing the brush to begin work.

How to use a brush correctly

Proper use of the brush is very important. (Keep the brush out of the mouth when using. This is an unsanitary, distasteful habit. Saliva in direct contact with the emulsion of color paper will work as a slow-acting acid.)

Always stroke a brush — never twist the hairs against their natural point. Prepare the brush before beginning work. Place the bristles in water and soften them with stroking movements. When soft, shape the point in the hand or on the wrist.

Step by step procedure for proper brush use

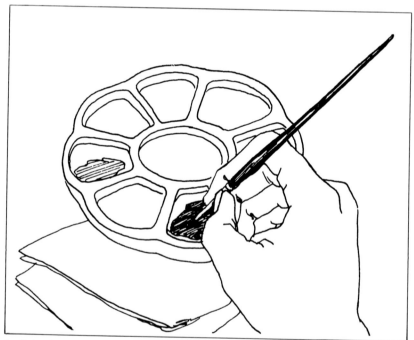

1. Saturate, until brush is filled with color needed.

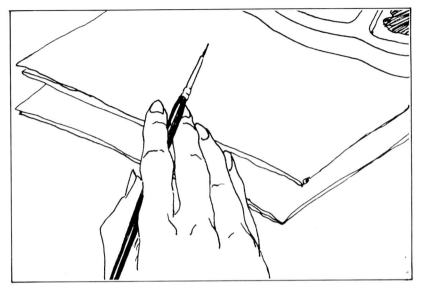

2. Wipe excess off on white tissue.

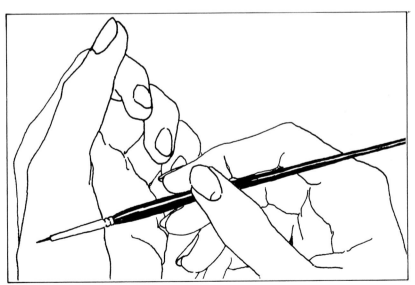

3. Point on wrist.

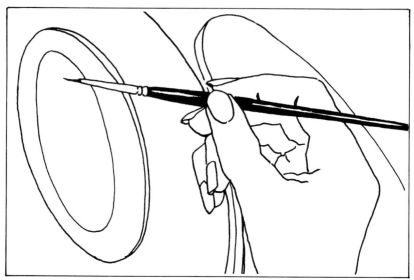

4. Work with tip of brush to release dye.

Brush tips and technique

Fanning The Brush

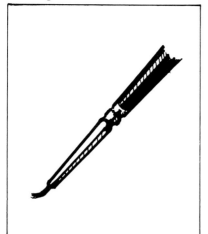

To fan a brush, bend sable hairs halfway, making them spread. This is used for a dye wash or to cover a wider area.

Brush tip — negative and print

A Wet Dry Brush

Dye in upper part of brush is wet. Hairs outside of brush are dry. Dye is released through tip or lead hair.

Facts about your brush

From the earliest days of art, when the cave dwellers of Lascaux decorated their walls with pictures of contemporary aminals, brushes have been used as the universal tools for the application of color.

Developing from simple bunches of animal hair or vegetable fiber, artists' brushes are now made in a wide variety of shapes and sizes from carefully selected materials; but each one is still made individually by hand. Modern techniques of mass production are employed for the manufacture of the handles and ferrules, but the brush itself is in every case the result of a brushmaker's skill and dexterity, working by the traditional method handed down from one generation of craftsmen to another.

All artists' brushes manufactured by Winsor & Newton, Ltd., are made throughout in their own modern factories at Wealdstone and Lowestoft, England. From small beginnings in 1879, when brushmaking was first added to the firm's activities, the department has grown to be the largest and best-known organization in the world devoted to the production of brushes for artists' use.

Today millions of brushes, each one individually hand-made and double-tested, go out to satisfy the needs of artists, designers, architects and students — pencils in sable and squirrel, lettering and one-strokes in sable and ox, oil color brushes of wide variety in sable and hog. Every brush is made from selected materials and each brush will give good service if properly treated.

Every possible care is take to maintain the highest standard of quality, but Winsor & Newton desire to make it clearly understood that it is the user's responsibility to make sure that the goods he purchases are suitable for his particular requirements. Also, Winsor & Newton can in no circumstance hold themselves responsible for any mishap that may arise from such particles as those of applying oil colors with the finger or putting water color brushes into the mouth.

Quoted from the Winsor & Newton, Inc., Catalog

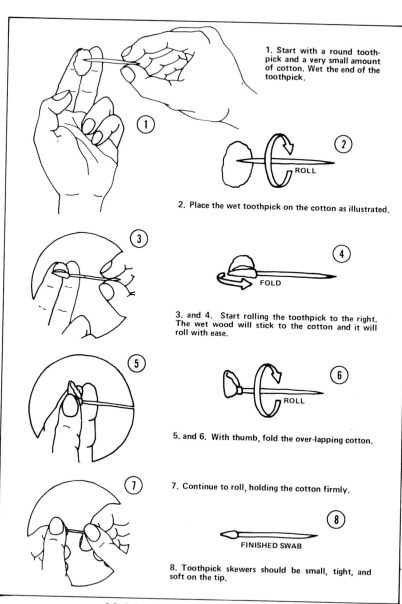

1. Start with a round toothpick and a very small amount of cotton. Wet the end of the toothpick.

ROLL

2. Place the wet toothpick on the cotton as illustrated.

FOLD

3. and 4. Start rolling the toothpick to the right. The wet wood will stick to the cotton and it will roll with ease.

ROLL

5. and 6. With thumb, fold the over-lapping cotton.

7. Continue to roll, holding the cotton firmly.

FINISHED SWAB

8. Toothpick skewers should be small, tight, and soft on the tip.

Making A Toothpick Skewer

CHAPTER SEVEN

There are little tricks to every trade

There are some little tricks to the retouching trade which can speed up work. My favorite is use of a common round toothpick. Make one or several cotton-tipped skewers with them to use for blending colored leads until they almost look like dyes. The skewers are also good for removing excess grains from graphite. Sometimes tiny dye spots can build up on the negative. This skewer method will also remove the dye specks.

How to make a toothpick skewer

1. Start with a round toothpick and a very small amount of cotton. Wet the end of the toothpick.
2. Place the wet toothpick on the cotton as illustrated.
3-4. Start rolling the toothpick to the right. The wet wood will stick to the cotton and it will roll with ease.
5-6. With thumb, fold the over-lapping cotton.
7. Continue to roll, holding the cotton firmly.
8. Toothpick skewers should be small, tight, and soft on the tip.

Working with toothpick skewer

When involved with graphite retouching and one spot contains too much lead, rather than cleaning the whole negative, try the following:

Take a bottle of retouching fluid and with the brush, dab a small amount on your wrist. Let is set during the time it takes to place cap back on the bottle. Next take toothpick skewer and lightly touch the spot dabbed on your wrist. Take a whiff of retouching fluid, touching only the area desired to be cleaned on the emulsion side. It will be cleaned by this method quickly and easily.

Another trick is removing graphite from the holder, permitting it to be held separately. I use HB, a double purpose lead. The H stands for hard, gray black lead and B is a soft, very black lead. They are ground together and blended.

Since I have a fine touch, I prefer not to use a holder for lead. I can perfectly control the lead with two fingers. To do so, hold lead with thumb and forefinger so that your finger is at least two inches from the tip. Do not apply pressure to the lead. Pleace the lead on the negative and guide it around. Weave the lead on the negative; the vibrator on the machine will make the texture. Use lead on the areas to which you can no longer add dye in both color and black and white.

CHAPTER EIGHT

Retouching a color negative

Retouching fluid, an important part of negative retouching, can cause many problems when applied incorrectly. With today's fine negatives, retouching fluid may not be needed. Try dye first. If it doesn't adhere well, then use fluid. Before applying retouching fluid, place the negative on clean, white paper. Never use a fibrous paper like newspaper, as it is too coarse and little specks that can't be seen will stick to the negative. Inexpensive white paper (8×11 sheets) is available from a print shop, which can be bound into tablets.

Dope (the common term for applying retouching fluid) all the negatives planned for the day's retouching on both sides. This is a time-saver. Work on both sides may not be necessary, but if it is, the negative will be ready. Wear a cotton or nylon glove while doing this, as it is important to avoid getting finger prints on the negative.

Another good reason to dope both sides of the negative is that the retouching fluid fills in the fine scratches often found on Veri-color negatives. Left uncovered, they .appear as soft white lines on the print, creating a spotting job, which results in loss of time and profit.

Materials needed for doping include cotton, glove, clean paper and retouching fluid.

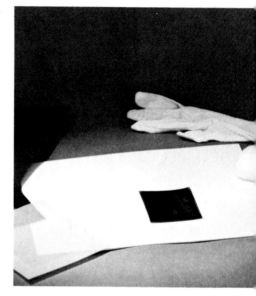

Apply fluid to center of negative, holding corner with gloved hand.

With large wad of cotton or tissue, wipe retouching fluid, using a circular motion, around the negative. Use this motion until completely dry.

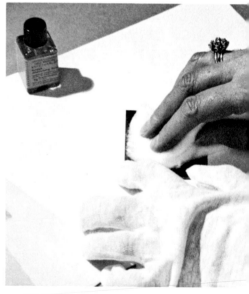

Apply a small amount of the fluid to the center of the negative or the subject's face. Place a large puff of cotton or a folded facial tissue on the fluid and spread it around in a circular motion, moving towards the edge of the negative.

Cotton is fine on unmasked negatives. When a negative already has a mask, it is better to use a soft, good quality tissue, preventing cotton fibers from sticking to the edge of the mask.

Don't press too hard while applying the fluid, but DO keep wiping constantly until the negative is smooth and not sticky. The finished negative should be very dry and look as though nothing is on it. Pressing too hard may cause the negative to bend; and once the negative is creased, it cannot be straightened out. The damage will have to be repaired on the print.

Retouching fluid is like a thin coat of glue. It provides a tooth on which the graphite can adhere, so that the lead won't brush off before printing. The fluid also creates a smooth base, allowing more control when using dyes with less chance of puddling. My personal choice is Kodak retouching fluid because it is consistent and never sticky.

A word of caution: Make sure that the cotton or tissue used is of the highest quality. It should be free of fibers or imperfections to avoid scratches on the negative. For years I recommended a brand of cotton, but recently small burrs have appeared on it. They are not big enough to scratch a human, but they are certainly large enough to scratch fine color negatives. I have discovered another type of cotton made especially for photography, Kendall Lakeside Cotton. It is long-fibered, soft, and safe.

There are times when a few slightly pink spots will appear over retouching while the rest of the negative is perfect. Here again, use a small skewer. Wet it slightly and then gently wipe the spot off on the base side of the negative.

When making corrections like this, the negative will appear terribly messy, but it will print just fine. The appearance of the negative can be cleaned by applying a second coat of retouching fluid over negative, then wiping it dry. The second doping will not change the corrected negative if the dye has been applied correctly. Be cautious — check the retouching anyway.

Special Note #1 Film, when properly developed, may not need retouching fluid. However, check the negative for fine scratches and —

don't forget — the retouching fluid fills in these minor scratches, and a softer base is inclined to scratch easily.

Special Note #2   Color identification is treated differently from black and white. Color is neutralized — black and white is etched.

4 x 5 Base Side

Making negative identifications — color

It is important to recognize the difference between the base and the emulsion side of the negative. The base is the preferred side for retouching. There the dye color is controlled and can be applied more heavily; there is a limited amount of diffusion, and you will be protecting the emulsion.

4×5 — The base side of 4×5 is notched on the left side. The printing appears on the emulsion side. Kodak, Agfa or foreign color film are standards. The base accepts dyes well and graphite can be used on the emulsion or base.

70mm (Roll film). There is an ID box on 70mm film at the bottom for numbers or name. The best way to identify this negative for base is by the code number found on the side of the negative. The code for 70mm is 21-07. This can be abraded, also.

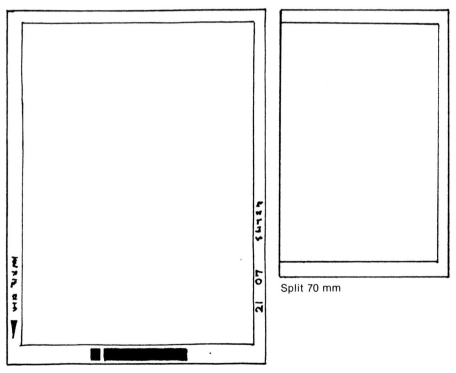

70 mm

Split 70 mm

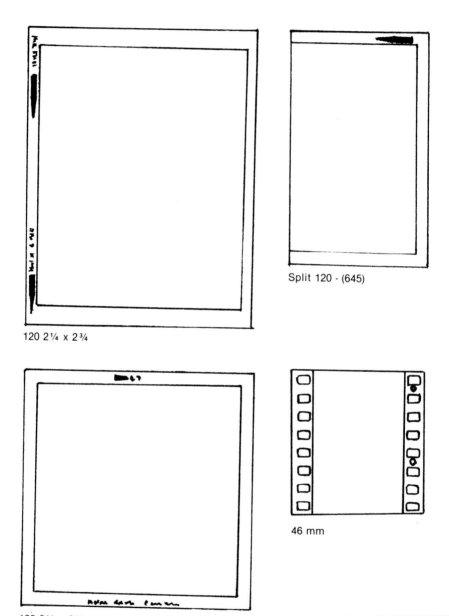

120 2¼ x 2¾

Split 120 - (645)

46 mm

120 2¼ x 2¼

Split 70mm. Sometimes this size negative has no numbers or writing on it because of the split. To identify the base side, take a wet toothpick skewer and touch both sides on the lower corner. Where the water leaves a dark mark, this is the emulsion side. The base side will show no mark.

120 — 2¼×2¾. You can read the words KODAK SAFETY FILM on the base side. This can be retouched with dye and graphite.

120 — 2¼×2¼. Smaller format but same film as 120 above.

120 split 2¼×2¾. Referred to as 645. This too is the same as 120 above.

46mm. This film is appearing in a few areas and is not designed to be retouched.

35mm. This is also not designed for retouching.

What colored leads are used for

A set of colored leads can be useful to the retoucher. A good set such as Staedtler should last a long time. A colored lead can solve unusual, difficult or simple problems. There are eight colors available in sets of 12. These include:

BROWN: Used for freckles and age spots, also for Spanish and Mexican comlexions.

YELLOW: For yellowed teeth or aged bruises.

CYAN: For an over-neutralized negative (this is a blue-green color).

GREEN: For unwanted green shadows caused by projected backgrounds, indoor gardens and clothings.

BLUE: For blue veins, blue beards and often new bruises; clothing.

RED or CARMINE: For blemished areas, scars, red eyelids, sores and bites and rashes.

PURPLE and VIOLETTE: Used for black complexions. There is enough red in this to neutralize, but if more is needed, add VCH dye over the purple lead.

ORANGE: For unwanted blue that might appear on Vericolor negative when finished. This often happens under eyes.

There is little chance of overdoing an art correction with colored leads. To use a colored lead, lightly apply over needed area, blending in with toothpick skewer (on emulsion side). Used properly, leads will appear as smooth as a dye on the print. If graphite needs to be added over the lead, it will be easy to do so as the base of this lead is not too greasy. Dye can be used over colored leads if necessary.

Masks for negatives

Masks serve several purposes for negatives, helping keep the negative clean and avoiding fingerprints. Their second purpose it to handle the negative when it is being placed in the negative cage of the retouching stand. The right size for the negative will also block out excess light. I have found that 4×5 brown Kraft negative preserves are excellent for making masks.

Many labs have designed masks to fit their own machine printers. The retoucher will often receive negatives already masked, which can be a real help. Just remember, when doping a negative in a mask, it is better to use facial tissue as lens cleaner as opposed to cotton which may stick inside the edge.

Study your proof

Learn to read the proof, as it will tell you where the corrections are needed. Form a good habit. Eyes should be trained to start in the same

A 4 x 5 brown Kraft negative preserve makes an excellent mask.
When doping a negative in a mask, use facial tissue as a cleaner, since cotton may stick inside of edge.

Study your proof to see correct color.

place each time a proof is studied. This way, a proof can be scanned with both speed and accuracy.

Determine the following:

What has to be retouched?
What needs neutralizing?
Where are the blemishes?
How bad are the circles under the eyes?
Check the hidden areas for faults.
What about blending and modeling? Are they needed?
Are there any hair corrections to be made?
What about age corrections.

Look for (1) hair corrections; (2) hot spots; (3) circles under eyes; (4) blemishes; (5) hidden faults.

The proof should look natural when finished. Character lines should be left, removing only the faults.

Retouching a color negative

Method 1 — DYE RETOUCHING   Since Vericolor film has come on the market, portraits and photographs are far more perfect, with little or no grain. The perfect way to retouch a negative is to do so leaving no graphite marks. Dye has been proven to do this successfully and is transparent. By applying dye as a transparent medium, just the flesh will remain and only the faults will be removed, resulting in a flawless print. In color the negative is neutralized. The dyes I speak about have balanced neutralizing color and density added. (VC colors.)

There are three main shades of dye available to cover specific areas: VC II is used for the highlight area, which is the darkest area on the negative, appearing dark red. VC Shadow I is for the mid-tones and circles under the eyes, and is also good on medium-dark skin. This will be a light-brownish color on the negative. VC Shadow II is designed to be used in the darkest areas which will be gray in color on the negative. It's good for glass shadows, moles and Adam's apples.

For particular problems, there are two additional dyes. VC Yellow is used to whiten teeth and on yellowed bruises and yellowed skins. Also excellent for yellow reflections in environmental color reflections (can be mixed with VC Shadow I or II or alone). VC Blue is used to neutralize pinkish tones on a negative.

Match the dye to the surrounding area so that print correction is kept at a minimum. To see color better, take a piece of developed white paper and place the colors of the dyes on the paper. Label each dye, then match to proof to make sure the correct color is being used.

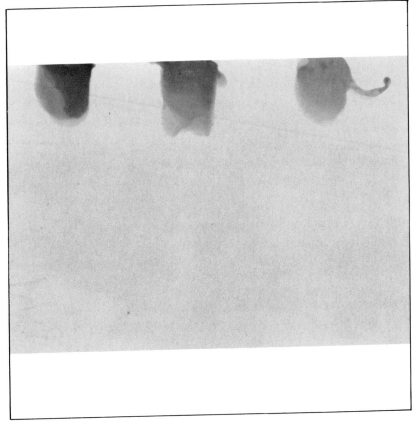

Dye color chart.

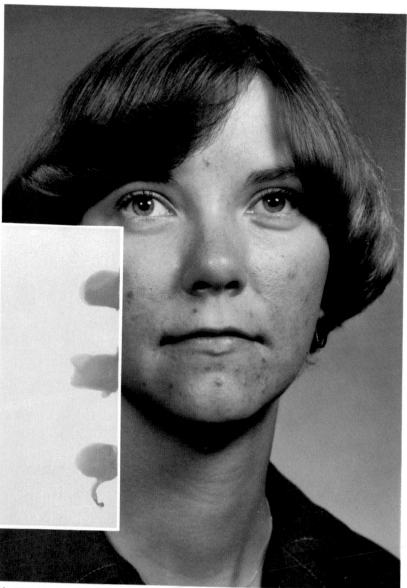

Unretouched print with color chart against face, comparing color. Blemishes are dark red like blemishes in highlight area. Middle tone (mid-face), actually the first shadow blemishes turn a brownish color. The neckline contains a third shade, which is a grayish color on lines in neckline area. Remember to remove only the unwanted color, not the flesh tone.

After negative is retouched with dye only. This print has not been spotted.

Method 2 Study the proof and negative to determine where red lead or dye needs to be applied. If you use red lead, be sure it has the right point — a blunt lead will not cover well. (See lead diagrams.)

The red lead or dye is used to neutralize. Apply red dye on the base side of the negative over all blemishes, slightly under the eyes, and very little on the area that looks brownish. Then turn negative over to the emulsion side and cover the areas where the red was applied with graphite to finish. Hold graphite very lightly or use a holder and balance it lightly. Many retouchers prefer 2H or 3H as it is a lighter shade and harder lead.

Hold red lead (or any colored lead) about an inch from the point because you need more pressure for color leads, as they are very soft. For graphite, see section on Black and White Retouching.

Preparation

When preparing for the day, arrange the negative orders in a stack and dope negatives in sequence. As each negative is doped, place it face down in order in a second rack. This is a good habit to develop as it is an easy way to keep track of the customer's work in case they should phone about their order.

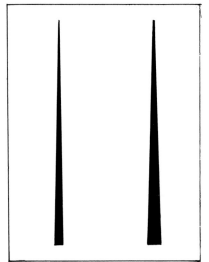

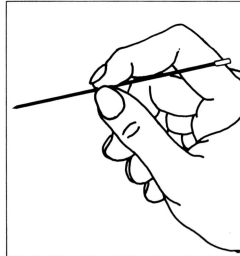

Graphite is sharpened fine, as shown above. Color is not sharpened as fine.

Hold lead gently between fingertips.

It's important to know the negatives, their sizes, what can be retouched and what cannot be retouched. Learn how to retouch the negative well. Following are the steps that should be taken.

1. Apply retouching fluid to both sides of the negative per instructions on retouching fluid application, page 47.
2. Place negative in a mask.
3. Slide mask into the negative cage on the retouching machine. Put the cage in the correct standing position. Base side of the negative should be face up.
4. Prepare the palette:
   a. Fill center of palette with water (distilled if possible).
   b. In one well, put enough VC II dye to cover bottom.
   c. Skip one well; in next well put some VC Shadow I. It is brownish in color.
   d. Skip another well and, in the next one, put in some VC Shadow II dye. This one is grayish in color.
   The wells skipped in between colors will be used for intermixing the colors. Other colors may be added to the palette as needed. Fold a white tissue and place it beneath the palette. Facial tissue is soft and will not wear out the brush.
5. Prepare the brush (see Section The Brush, page 39).

When the negatives are finished and readied for retouching, be sure all of the tools are prepared. While the dyes are fresh, test a spot of color on the white sheet of paper in front of the machine. This is how the dye is kept consistent in color. Don't forget — as time passes, evaporation will take place and dyes will thicken, which can cause problems. Keep a little plastic drip bottle with water by the palette, which will allow a drop at a time to be added to the dye, preventing over-dilution.

When inserting the negative into the cage of the machine, the cage handle should be in a downward position. When inserting the masked negative, the eyes of the subject should be horizontal with the handle of the cage. This makes it easier to work with the contour of the face.

Now, retouching of the negative can begin.

1. Prepare the brush by saturating it with water. Wipe off excess water on tissue. (To soften brush before beginning to retouch — not necessary to be done each time.)

2. Saturate brush next with dye, again wiping excess dye on the tissue. Wipe the brush by holding it in an almost horizontal position so that all of the dye is not released from the brush, but instead trapping dye in the brush hairs. The inside will be wet and the outside will be dry to the touch.
3. For a good point or tip, stroke brush across lower thumb area or wrist. The warmth of the flesh will put hairs in place. If dye should come off, it is too wet.
4. With left hand, control the negative cage. Turn the arm toward the top of the machine. This will put negative in proper position for retouching.
5. Machine should be turned on with vibrator geared to negative size. (See page 34.)
6. Apply dye to the forehead first, working with the tip of the brush. Do not bend tip too much, and do not dab . . . stroke.
7. Start by using this method. There are, however, other methods which will be discussed later. Start with the VC II dye to do most of the retouching, especially in highlight areas. Flow dye on by placing tip of brush on the line or spot and move the brush just slightly back and forth. Flow in until the spot disappears and blends in with the surrounding area.
8. If there is blending to be done, dilute the VC II dye.
9. Should you need a medium shade, use VC Shadow I in the midtone area.
10. If the spot is very red on the proof, and appears very green on the negative, blend with the VC II with red dye.
11. When working in the deeper shadows or necklines, use VC Shadow II. Sometimes reflecting colors create deeper shadows under eyes and Shadow II would also be needed there.
12. Study the proof — see the different colors.

Working with contour of face

It is important to work with the contour of the face for many reasons. The brush will stay in line better, and will be following a natural flow. Where there are lines on forehead and neck, the subject is sideways and the brush will stay in line better by working down.

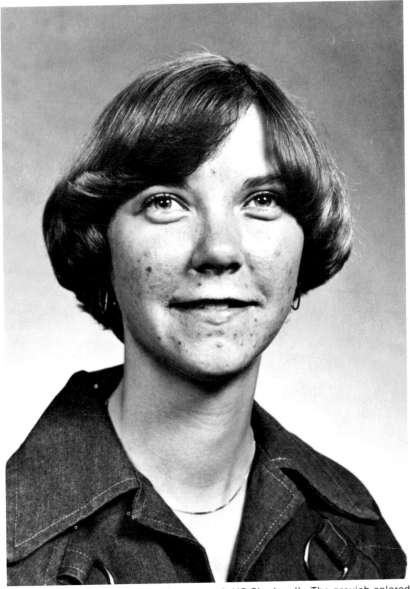

Before and After. Retouched with
1. VCII - The reddish colored dye, used on blemishes in highlight.
2. VC Shadow I - The brownish colored dye, used under eyes and in midtones of face.

3. VC Shadow II - The grayish colored dye, used on deepest shadow and where blue reflects. Also used on necklines.
No graphite was used.

When retouching the neckline or any other facial line, make small strokes going down the line. It will fill in better. Use only the tip of the brush, using small movements. Make strokes not dabs, for a natural looking print, which is the reason dye retouching is so superior.

When the negative is completed, take a piece of blue acetate and view the negative through it. The clear blue acetate will show if the spots are completely retouched. The negative will not be perfectly smooth as there may be a light spot here or there. Carefully look for all of these light spots and retouch them. This will make a real difference between an accomplished retoucher and a proof retoucher.

Tip in negative retouching

If, while working on the base side of a negative with dye, too much is applied, it can be removed with standard household ammonia. Apply a little to a toothpick skewer and rub the base gently.

CHAPTER NINE

Retouching black and white negatives

In black and white retouching, we are working with tones — blacks to greys, and tones can also be removed by etching. The supplies needed to retouch black and white negatives are: retouching machine or stand, elbow pads, doping pad, retouching fluid, lamp, graphite (HB — hard and soft lead mixed) or 2H, 3H to 2B, sandpaper #360 waterproof, etching knife (Adams), VC Shadow II, opaque, cotton, emery polishing paper, auto state, masks in three sizes and an abrading needle.

Steps to follow:

1. Apply retouching fluid over emulsion side of the negative completely. Do not streak on emulsion side.
2. View the negative. Look for hair corrections. Make a mask to suit the negative — large enough to check the hair. Correct the hair first. Does it need graphite? If so, where? Does it need etching? Where? Does it need dye? Does it need the abrading tool?
3. Turn vibrator on 20 for black and white negatives, 70mm, 90mm and 4×5. For 120 negatives turn vibrator to 10.
4. Retouch small hair corrections with graphite. If hair strands are too fine, use the abrading needle. When there is void space in the hair

arrangement, use the etching knife. Fill in the hair openings by following the hair contour. Keep in line so you have a natural look when finished.

5. When working, turn the negative, working with the contour of the face as with color negatives. Clean (retouch) hair first, forehead, right (or left side) and nose, chin, neck, left side. Then sit back slightly and view to see if it is blended.

6. To speed up retouching and make a smoother finish, dye the negative on the base side with dark dye. This will cover most of the larger areas and then use graphite on the emulsion side to blend and finish where the dye could not cover.

7. Blending. This is important for a professional finish. Do most of the blending with dye. Basically, this mixes everything together smoothly and inseparably to intermix, tying all the artwork together and making the negative smooth and beautiful. Where should blending occur? The spot and areas that are very faint and difficult to see. Move the magnifying glass away — this will show the light areas that may have been missed.

8. Check negative for pinholes — if visible, use the abrading tool to correct. If there are scratches on the negative, use opaque; or if there are stains, use dye to fix troubled area.

How to use the abrading tool

The abrading tool is a metal holder with a sharp needle. It is valuable if used properly. Steps for proper usage are:

1. Use on negative base side only. Hold needle at a 90 degree angle. Abrading tool can be used on a color or a black and white negative. Turn the vibrator up to 50.

2. Just touch base over area that has flaw. Do not press too hard. Touch 3 or 4 times, it depends on what the problem is — hair or pinhole. Hold the needle close to the negative and let the retouching machine vibrator do the work. Keep the needle close to be more accurate.

3. Light from the enlarger bounces around and through and acts like a prism, reflecting unwanted spots or lines out and has the same effect

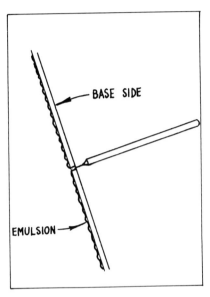

The Abrading Tool.

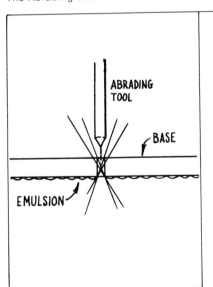
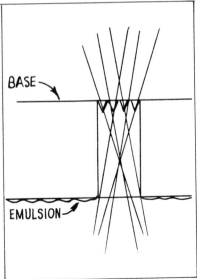

as lead on the emulsion. This type of retouching will print heavier than it appears to the eye. Therefore, I recommend that this be under-done.

If green should appear when abrading is done, turn to the emulsion side and use red lead or red dye. (Color negative.)

Uses for abrading tool Abrading tools are used for hair corrections, pinholes or other minute spots and line and for small negatives with small head sizes, where there are fine lines under the eyes.

The etching knife for black and white retouching

There are several brands of etching knives on the market. Among them are those made by Adams and Kodak. These are fine tools be to used on black and white negatives. They remove the emulsion from the negative, thus removing density so that light can come through. They are good for correcting hair, clothing, reflection in eyes, glares on glasses and for restoration of negatives. Etching can be easily done on 5×7, 4×5, 70mm, and 90mm negatives but is not advisable for 120 negatives.

The etching knife should be held as pictures. (See #1.) For working in small areas, hold at 90° angle and work with the point. For large corrections, drop back onto the heel to cut a wider area. Move with a natural stroke. I work with an upward movement most of the time; but in certain spots, I find it necessary to stroke down.

Touch the knife to the negative very lightly and scrape the emulsion slowly. This is a skill with which you have to be patient. Keep the vibrator on 10 or 15. The machine will feather the edges as you stroke.

See illustration #2 for position of knife for fine line or small area and illustration #3 for knife for wider areas.

Take care of a good knife. Keep it in a drawer covered with the tip protector when not in use. After the etching tool, you may sometimes see some lines showing. When printed, there then will be too much contrast.

To prevent this from happening, turn to the base of the negative. Directly over the area etched, rub in an abrasive reducer or a soft eraser. This will cause a diffusion. Sometimes a little graphite correction may be needed.

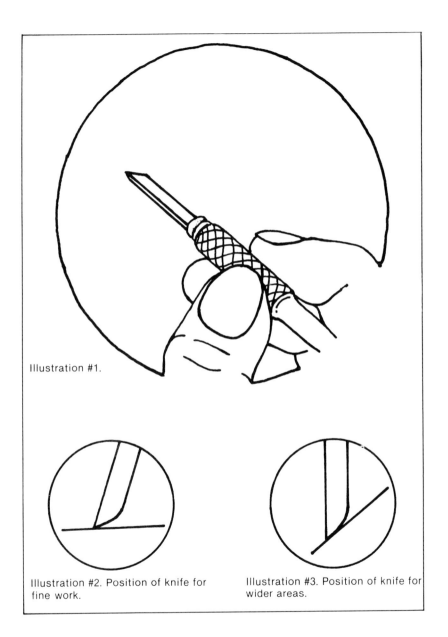

Illustration #1.

Illustration #2. Position of knife for fine work.

Illustration #3. Position of knife for wider areas.

The Don't's of Etching
1. Do not etch color negatives.
2. Do not loan the etching knife.
3. Do not use etching knife for other purposes.

Sharpening the Knife To sharpen the knife, use emery polishing paper. Pull the knife across the paper three or four times away from the body and then back once. Do this to both edges on the Adams knife. Do the same with the Kodak knife, just on the one edge.

How to wash a negative

When too much dye has been applied to a negative, it is necessary to wash the negative. This is a fairly easy job. The water used must be lukewarm (approximately 76 °F). The pan should be raised slightly on one end so that when the water pours in at the corner, it will create a swirl, causing the excess water to pour off (see sketch).

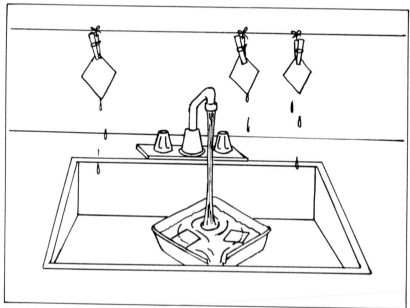

Washing the negative.

Place negatives in the pan. Let the water run into the pan from the faucet at a medium-slow speed. Turn it off after five minutes, add a few drops of Photo-Flo and swish negatives around slightly. Hang negative up to dry by the corner. Photo-Flo prevents water marks.

When negatives are dry, they may look messy since the water will have removed all of the dye. Further clean the negative with anti-stat film cleaner to remove all of the old retouching fluid and lead that has remained after the wash. Apply retouching fluid again and start retouching.

Opaquing a negative

A scratched negative can often be saved by opaquing. It is easier to correct a print with a white spot or line but much more difficult to cover a black mark. The tools needed for opaquing are: Speed-o-paque or Kodak spotting colors, and a #178-0000 Grumbacher brush.

Put a small amount of water in an empty well in the retouching palette. Never use the same water which has been used with the dye brush. With a fine brush and Kodak spotting colors or Grumbacher's Speed-o-paque, a fine line can be made on the base side of the negative directly over the scratch. Explain in a note to the printer that the negative has been opaqued so that the darkroom will not clean off the negative.

Make a paste of the opaque using a wet brush. Pick it up with the brush and quickly apply it to the negative base side for a smooth line. Practice a few times on the side of the negative. If it has been applied incorrectly, remove it, using a wet toothpick skewer. Wet the opaque spot and simply lift off by touching with the wet toothpick.

For opaquing larger areas, use Kodak commercial opaques or Grumbacher's opaques with a larger brush, such as a Grumbacher #178-1 or #178-2. This can be used for opaquing out a background or for bringing out an individual person for reproduction.

When outlining a person's head on a small negative, do not get too close to the head. I have found that it is easier to finish the outline on a print, as there is less chance of changing the head size when the negative has been printed.

CHAPTER TEN

What to look for in retouching different age groups

In retouching *baby* pictures, look at temple bone structure; crying eyes; reddish-brown circles; rash on cheeks; drool on chin-shadows; drool on clothing — density spots; bruises; insect bites and dirty shoes.

Pre-teen portraits from First Communion and Confirmation should be checked for minor blemishes, scratches, fatigue lines and heavy circles and bruises.

Senior portraits should be viewed for circles under eyes, fatigue lines, blemishes, blending and minor hair corrections.

In doing *glossies for publication*, look for general retouching needs, check blue beards. Do not change characteristics of the person. If the subject is a man, leave masculine. If a woman, leave feminine.

Portraits of *individuals in their 40's* should be checked for lines between eyebrows and dry skin lines. Be diplomatic; people of this age group feel strong and good and want to look young. Check the neckline and make sure it looks pleasing.

For *Golden Age* portraits, soften all lines. Remove vertical lines around the mouth, correct necklines as much as possible. Watch the sagging jowl line. In order to keep the natural contour, there has to be print corrections in that area.

Some other general areas to look for in retouching are: minor hair corrections; the forehead, look for blemish in hairline, on eye brows and smooth out highlight on forehead. Check the chin and neck. Keep the character of the chin, just remove blemishes and blend. Leave cleft in chin. In the neck remove lines; leave the shadow alone and check for blemishes.

Look at the right side of the face, the shadow side. Retouch under the eyes; retouch all blemishes and light grey spots and be sure to match to surrounding areas. Leave some shadowing under eye. Check hidden areas for blemishes, and then remove fatigue lines.

On the left side of the face, remove fatigue line under eye. Soften circle under eye, blemishes and blending same as other side. Always look

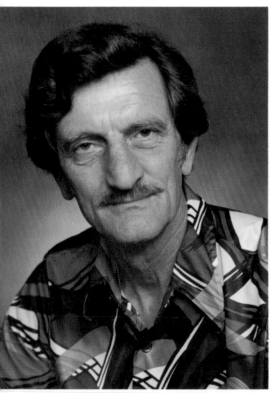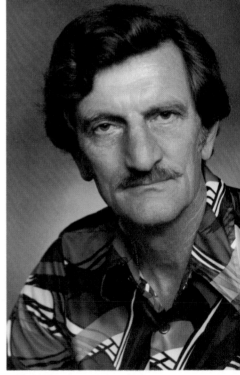

Before and After. Lines softened with VCII, VC Shadow I and VC Shadow II. No graphite was used. Prints have not been spotted or corrected in any way. Lines have just been softened.

for unwanted and out-of-place shadow under the nostril.

Let's discuss the various age groups independently.

Babies do need retouching

I find it frustrating to hear a photographer, receptionist or retoucher to say, "Oh, we don't retouch babies, they're perfect." Babies do need to be retouched. Following is a list of the items to look for requiring retouching:

1. The shape of the head. Many times a child is born under difficult circumstances, and the bone form may be out of shape at the temple. When photographed, this head will give a square appearance. Soften the area with dye, and round out the temple or at least make it less obvious.
2. Babies cry, especially when their routine is broken. As a result, they will most likely have circles under their eyes or the photographer's lighting may darken the circles. Shadow II dye can help correct this.
3. Many babies have rashes on their cheeks. The VC II dye or carmine red lead will remove this beautifully on the base side of the negative or carmine can be used on the emulsion side.
4. Drooling — a single drop may be cute but more than this may be displeasing so retouch area as you see fit.
5. Mosquito bites are noticeable and should be removed.
6. During their curiosity time, babies are subject to bruises. Keep aware of this; look for bruises as you prepare to retouch baby portraits.
7. Check shoes. Toes may be dirty from crawling.

Retiring Age Portraits

At retiring age, age should be respected. Retouch on base side. Soften all lines until not obvious. Remove vertical lines around mouth and shorten lines from mouth to chin. Do as much as possible on the neck. By doing this on the base side, it has a diffused effect when printed, reducing the age lines to a soft effect without over-retouching.

4. Twinkle in the eyes, sometimes called "crow's feet." These should be softened. Do not remove this look or it will dull the eyes and take away from the expression.
5. Shape of nose. Do not highlight or change shape. Just remove spots and marks.
6. Cheek lines, all are individual. Over-retouching will change individual's facial structure and widen face.
7. Lips — leave the vertical lines and remove the horizontal lines that indicate dryness. Do not over-retouch.
   Chine — (space between lip and chin), do not change. The shadow in this area is different on every person. Leave cleft.
9. Adam's Apple. Just soften this area.
10. Dimples. Do not remove these in portraits.
11. Birthmarks. Have the receptionist discuss this with the customer. It can be a touchy problem.
12. Freckles. Leave these on color negative; just break up the clusters and soften the dark ones. Black and white — remove as much as possible as they appear as dirty spots.

Before and After of Retiring Age Portrait. All lines softened, reducing age lines without over-retouching.

How to retouch character lines and marks to project person's image

The camera captures the character of people. There are features which distinguish one person from another. The retoucher must be careful not to destroy these through over-retouching. Following is a list of features and an explanation of what should or should not be done in retouching these areas.

1. Moles. Unless customer requests these be removed, leave the prominent, dark brown moles on. Softening can be done if too obvious.
2. Type of grin or smile. Do not change or remove a person's smile. If lighting is too harsh, soften.
3. Lines on forehead, especially noticeable with young people. Deep, fleshy lines are expressive and often heriditary. Just soften.

CHAPTER ELEVEN

Negative retouching problems — how to correct them

In working with negatives, several problems may develop. Some result from improperly developed film. This causes the negatives to lose tooth and makes it difficult to get lead to adhere. This is just one problem; others, which may be encountered are discussed below:

Scratches on negatives

There are four general types of scratches appearing on negatives:

1. Very fine scratches. To correct, apply retouching fluid to both sides of negative.
2. A definite scratch (like a hair or dust line). This can be abraded.
3. The large scratch (a gouge on the emulsion). This type should be opaqued on the base side of the negative.
4. The long vertical or horizontal scratch caused by processing or by the camera. This scratch will be on the base side of the negative and appear white on the print. Use an ordinary pencil eraser to gently erase down the line on the base side. This will diffuse the scratch. Be sure the eraser is clean and not made of abrasive rubber. Clean off grit with a toothpick skewer, then apply retouching fluid. Although the eraser method can diffuse scratch to some extent, it may still show as a faint line on the print but is easy to correct with dyes. Color scratches will have to be finished on print.

Tinted glasses

Tinted glasses on color negatives can sometimes create a color problem. Take the negative color chart with VC Retouching dyes and compare it to the tint. Apply that color to the entire glass area, going over the eyes and everything else to remove just the tint. Mix VC II and VC Shadow I to make the rose-brown effect. For the smokey shade, Shadow II will do. Finish retouching the circles under the eyes. VC yellow sometimes has to be added to Shadow I for yellowish-brown tinted glasses. When unwanted color is removed, then retouch fatigue lines and circles under eyes.

Damaged negatives

A damaged negative that has many pinholes or small scratches can be saved. Try the abrading needle first on the base side of the negative. Touch slightly over the area (see directions page 68). If the hole or scratch is too large, opaque the negative with a fine brush. This should be done before dying negative or use graphite.

Thin negatives

A thin negative, that is too light but has potential possibilities can and should be done mainly with dyes, using a slightly diluted dye. Work from the base side. You can also build highlights and reduce shadows using dark dye. Graphite should not be used to finish a thin negative, it will show.

Dense negatives

A dense negative is one that is too dark. The dark areas can easily be retouched, but the circles under the eyes or bad blemishes that show up white will be more difficult to cover. A proof should be used for these and studied before doing any retouching. Both sides may have to be worked. For black and white, dye base side using Shadow II, on the emulsion side use graphite. With a dense negative, it is important to have a good light to see that all corrections are made. For color use, Shadow I and II mixed together. Turn machine light on to full brightness.

Glasses

Several problems can be caused by glasses. Glares on glasses in color negatives cannot be retouched correctly. This must be done on the print. The refraction of flesh in glasses occur if background is compatible; here you can blend to an extent. This is most often a print correction. Another concern is plastic-framed glasses. These leave a large shadow and also pick up color. The customer should be told that shadows like these are natural. Some shadows can, however, be toned down slightly with dye. Avoid using graphite, it shows grain on the finished print when applied in dense areas. For black and white, glares can be etched and shadows dyed.

Retouching without proofs

It is a problem for the retoucher to try to retouch without proofs or previews. To do qualified retouching, a retoucher needs to read the color in order to remove faulty colors. The proof serves as a guideline and is therefore a necessity.

Retouching under eyes

For black and white: To retouch under eyes there are two types of material that can be used . . . graphite and dyes. To retouch with graphite, turn negative so that eyes are sideways for free movement. On the emulsion side of the negative make fine criss-cross lines under the eyes (the circle) and fatigue lines. This will print more like a flesh texture. Fill in light area, letting just enough light come through so that a soft shadow will still appear under eyes when negative is printed.

Turn the negative sideways, following the natural flow of the contour lines on face. If eyelid is green on negative, use red dye or carmin lead to correct.

83

For color: If you prefer, you can retouch with dyes by turning the negative sideways to follow the natural flow of contour lines on the face. If the eyelid appears green on the negative, use red dye or carmine lead to correct it. (See diagram.)

Pull brush down with a natural wrist movement. Start with the tip and slightly fan the brush as the space or line becomes wider. Shadow I dye should work perfectly; sometimes colors from clothing or background pick up greys or blues and reflect under the eyes. If negative has slightly reddish cast, use the VC blue. This would appear as a highlight.

How to retouch blemishes

Negative with blemish.

Negative after retouching.

Proof of negative with blemish before retouching.

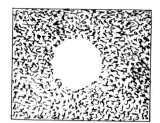

1. This is what a blemish looks like on a negative.

2. Start on inside edge of blemish or small spot and blend towards center. Turn vibrator on (10 to 15 for color, 15 to 20 for black and white) the graphite will automatically texture. Dyes blend much easier.

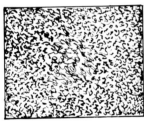

3. A finished spot should look like this — matched to the surrounding area.

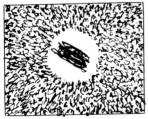

4. *Do not* dab in the center of the spot (blemish). It is too difficult to match skin texture and often is not finished.

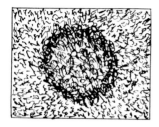

5. Do not overlap. It will leave a ring around the blemish, and create a spotting problem. This will print too white around the blemish and make it stand out.

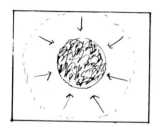

6. Blending on a negative — ususally on an uneven skin caused by acne or a mild case of blemishes. I've just told you about retouching a blemish and yet there are times — even when you've done this correctly — that there is still a roughness to the facial area. Why? Well, the blemish is like a wound causing the surrounding area to flatten with fluid leaving to heal the wound. This gives the complexion an uneven appearance.

What you have done is match to that healing area and now you must blend to the normal skin. This can be done by diluting your dye (the color that matches in the area) and cover the entire area (meaning, the blemish and flattened skin).

How to correct a receded tooth

A receded tooth can be corrected on the negative. Working on the emulsion side, apply yellow lead to the entire tooth. Blend with a toothpick skewer, then highlight tooth with a small line of graphite. The amount of highlighting will depend upon where the tooth is located. On the base side apply "DARK" dye to the entire tooth until it matches both sides.

It is more difficult to correct a void tooth on a negative. The formula for fixing a receded tooth is generally accurate. A receded tooth is very often a brownish-gray. The brown is a yellow-brown. For yellowed teeth, a light wash of VC yellow dye should be applied. Be sure it is a light yellow — too much will cause purple teeth on print.

A new method is to mix VC yellow dye with either Shadow I or Shadow II, depending on density of discoloration. Apply to base side until teeth appear matched.

Retouching dark-skinned people

For light-skinned black people, use VC II in highlights and purple lead in shadows, deep blemishes and under eyes. For medium-skinned black people, use VC Shadow I in highlights and VC Shadow II in shadows and under the eyes. For very dark-skinned black people, use Shadow I in highlight areas and Perigrey in shadows and under eyes.

For yellow-colored skins, add VC yellow to the shadow dyes.

For red-colored skins, use Verona Brown.

Working with small negatives

In working with small negatives, the heads of subjects become very small. There is a limit to what can be seen on these, even when using magnifying and retouching glasses. Dyes are generally used.

Poorly arranged hair and bad complexions

A retoucher can only go so far in correcting hair or complexions or will cause bigger problems for the print retoucher. It is quicker and more efficient for these problems to be solved in front of the camera. (*See directions for these on page 11.*)

The heavy rush season

During the heavy rush season it is difficult for both the studio and the retoucher. This is the time when all the problem complexions come in.

On a badly blemished face, the negative will take the retoucher more time to correct than it does the photographers, receptionist and spotter all together. Just a touch of makeup would speed things up and also present a better proof.

Neutralizing

One major problem in color is neutralizing. When prints come back from the lab or the printer, the areas needing neutralizing may have turned green or blue. This may be caused by several factors. To determine the problem:

1. Check the background. Is the color correct? Look at the shadows in the neck and in the shadow area of the face. Is there blue or green in the darkness of the shadow?
2. If the background is off color, too much blue, cyan or green, then the printer is probably at fault.
3. If the background is correct then you may have over-neutralized or just removed the denisty of the problem and didn't neutralize.

To correct an over-neutralized area on print, use the VC method. Use a wet dry brush, number 2 Winsor Newton and VC spotting color peach, spot and blend in greenish area. The problem can be solved in a matter of seconds.

Improper training on negatives can also cause problems. Color retouching is much different than black and white. Proper training is needed to see through color and learn the dye method. Sometimes retouchers take accounts and never check on their work or just assume that color can be done like black and white.

Untrained retouchers often retouch in areas not needed in color. Very few retouchers can handle the smile line in a expert manner. Color shadows are not as offensive as black and white. When using graphite in this area of nose shadows, the finished product will often look very grainy. The head size is so small on a colored negative that when enlarged, it can't be helped but to look grainy. Dye can tone down but must be done correctly.

In working with leads, sharpness is a necessity. A dull lead will cause a grainy look. Also a dull point will overlap an imperfection, leaving a light ring around, and not completely covering, a blemish.

Dyes must be used properly or they cause problems. If you let dyes evaporate without diluting, you will over-neutralize. Using the wrong brush can cause sloppy retouching; using the brush wrong, causes over-neutralizing and other problems.

Yet another problem is trying to retouch in improper lighting. It cuts the retouching down and half the retouching can be missed by inability to see it.

A final problem is using a hard lead on a color negative. This prevents heavy retouching but causes under-retouching, appearing to need modeling.

PART 3

Print retouching

As a photographer, you are an artist who creates beautiful photographs, using your camera as a brush and capturing the likeness you desire. Nature sometimes creates little problems in the background or with the color desired. This is a simple matter to correct — you can change, enhance, improve, so many things. There are many mediums to do this today and also several little tricks that help increase speed, saving time and money, which is extremely important.

There is a beautiful satisfaction when you not only take the photograph but also print, retouch, art correct and finish, mastering the complete photograph.

Once you know what to do and how to do it, you can guide and teach others what can and cannot be done. Print correction begins with the emulsion of the print, the simple spotting.

There is something you may be unaware of in spotting. Quite often negatives are sent to be printed that have been retouched to the best of your ability — and sometimes, that's not all too great. It is the policy of many labs to do your spotting, and when poor retouching comes through, they spend a great deal of time covering up your mistakes, wanting prints to look good. After all, the print represents the lab, too.

They feel that if they do a good job for you, even in spotting, they can keep you as a customer and help you grow because your prints have been pleasing to the customer.

Spotting, the beginning of a good professional print, is hiding the white specks all over the print and sometimes the black specks. It is a professional MUST in the competitive field of photography.

There are times when a negative is too small to completely retouch, and there are times when a particular type of complexion will pick up several highlights. Because older people have so many character lines, it is often difficult to correctly retouch on the negative. These are the times when you print retouch. With a wet-dry brush and pre-mixed colors the job is simple, fast and effective to do.

With print retouching you can blend beautifully, but be careful not to over-retouch. It's important to retain the character and dignity of the subject.

CHAPTER TWELVE

How to spot professionally

To begin to spot, first prepare the palettes. The supplies needed are: two 8 × 10 pieces of glass, masking tape, two 8 × 10 pieces of white cardboard or paper, pure retouching colors (without density), Veronica's spotting colors. Or simpler yet, VC spotting palette — everlasting. (See sketch for size.)

Take an 8 × 10 piece of white cardboard and write or type the names of the colors in a convenient arrangement. For flesh, put brown, orange, red and yellow on right side of the palette and in the middle of the warm colors put neutral. On the left side of the palette, put cool colors — magenta, blue, green and cyan with neutral in the center. This will serve as your palette. I have noted neutral twice, because it is used so often for density. Each color belongs in it's proper place.

Next prepare the pre-mixed spotting paper. There are six colors, premixed to match today's photography: peach, tawny, verona brown, sepreen, perigrey and midnight on the other side.

Now two sheets are ready. Place an 8 × 10 piece of glass over each sheet and tape the edges of the palette with masking tape. I suggest an 8 × 10 piece of corrugated cardboard behind it to cushion the palette. When paper, board and glass are taped together, put liquid colors on the marked areas.

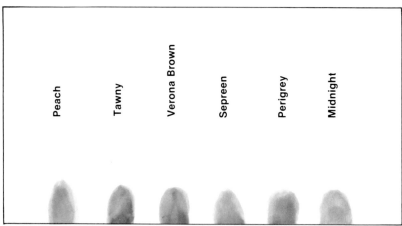

There are six colors used in spotting. Be sure to have colors run to the edge of the sheet of paper, allowing no gap to occur. (Use white process paper.)

Why should two palettes be used? Two reasons: first, I use pre-mixed colors for speed because they match so well. They blend well with subtle shades of color often found in portraiture photography. These colors are pre-mixed and ready to use directly on the print for portrait work and production spotting. They prefectly match the facial tones and backgrounds, already have density and are neutralized. There is no guess work using them.

Also needed is a palette of pure colors, which help create the brighter shades. For example, to spot a very blue sky, add either blue or cyan to perigrey. If the color is yellow, add either a cool or warm shade — whatever your black mask shows. This palette is good for neutralizing in commercial or outdoor photography.

Keep the palettes clean, dust and contamination free. If one of the two palettes is used more than the other, keep the other palette covered when not in use, avoiding a serious problem. A palette can become contaminated especially when a stabilizer brush is used often. Just imagine what happens when prints are out for a while then develop red specks, especially in areas that have been spotted. They have been contaminated and the cyan has been eaten away.

The prepared dye palette should also be kept clean. This dye is designed to be applied directly into the emulsion. Since this is prepared color, it should be put on the palette fresh everyday and only in the amount needed. This can be easily done as these new dyes have an eyedropper in each bottle.

Due to the new two-step chemistry in printing, stabilizer is no longer needed in spotting water. The prepared dyes are to be applied directly. (You may still want to use a stabilizer solution if you know that it was added as a last step in printing even though that lab or studio is using the 2-step chemistry.)

Use distilled water in the art department. It is both safe and inexpensive. Chemical reactions may take place when tap water is used for simple spotting.

Make a black mask with a small hole in the center about the size of a pea. Use this for seeing the color you need, placing the mask over the area needing spotting. By blocking out the surrounding area, you can see the real shade needed. There will be no close strong influence of other color misleading your eyes.

Place black mask over area to be spotted. The black mask will void unwanted color and show only color needed.

Make or purchase a spotting board that is portable.

A good size for the spotting board is 18" x 24", with a wide lip on bottom to hold print or tools. Have solid base for firmness.

A general spotting board layout, and also an art correction board.

Spotting should be situated conveniently for speedy efficiency. A tilted spotting board is needed for proper perspective and to prevent backaches, as is a good light for indoor and outdoor lighting. Cover board with white paper.

The white paper suggested is heavy "butcher" paper and is good for checking dye and pencil colors, for sharpening Prismas, mixing acrylics, for airbrush testing, and cleaning and wiping brushes on.

The spotting palette can be placed on the board also or on the table close by. I keep the two palettes in a convenient spot. Each person adopts a different arrangement to suit the area and for convenience.

The wet-dry brush method is as follows: Wet the brush completely with water. Wipe off extra water on facial tissue in side strokes. Point brush on wrist. This is to keep wetness inside and the hair on the outside almost dry. For Kodak color, smear around the desired colors and mix with other colors as needed.

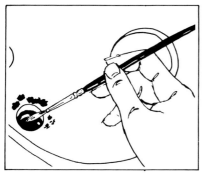 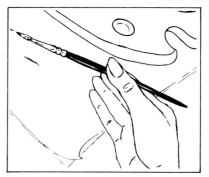

Saturate brush with dye bringing some out around the edges of the well for concentrated color.

Wipe excess dye off brush on white tissue.

For the prepared colors, saturate brush in fresh color, wipe dry in side-way strokes and test color on white paper. Be sure dye flow is regulated in strokes on white processed and then apply to print in the needed area.

I have developed a set of spotting colors, designed to simplify spotting on color prints. The colors are subtle and easy to blend in facial areas, hair, clothing or backgrounds.

The colors are:

Peach	Excellent for neutralizing over-neutralized prints (in negative retouching). Used in highlight areas or pink clothing.
Tawny	The perfect flesh tone for apricot or orange-toned photographs and also good on red areas, such as sunsets.
Verona Brown	Deep shadows in facial areas; glares on glasses; backgrounds in any brown area. Excellent for brown toned prints.

Sepreen	A neutral mixture between sepia and green — will
Perigrey	Excellent for blended backgrounds and for retouching black people on negatives.
Midnight	A dark shade for many spots.
VC Yellow	Subtle enough to blend with any yellow and also used on negative retouching..
VC Blue	Good for skies and brighter clothing. It is dulled just enough to blend well. Also for negatives used on negative retouching.

Directions for use of spotting colors

Place black spotting mask over area needing spotting. By blocking out the rest of the photograph you can quickly determine the shade needed. Make a small chart of spotting colors, using white process paper. Place colors on edge of paper — run chart next to hole in black mask. It will show the color needed.

Use a Winsor & Newton CO or #2 series 7 brush for spotting. Size depends on the area needing spotting. Check flow of brush and color on developed white paper. Drop dyes on a white palette and use wet-dry brush, working with just point of brush. If it evaporates, add a few drops of water to dilute.

Dye print retouching

Dyes can be used in the following areas:

a. on forehead, to tone down the highlight lines
b. between the eyes, to soften squint
c. under the eyes, to soften the white lines
d. on cheeks, chin and neck to soften all the white lines

All of the lighter areas should be done first. Working into the mid-tones, pick up Verona brown. It may be necessary to mix the tawny and Verona brown.

Going into the darkest areas, use the mask to assure the right color. If a bluish color appears from reflections, use the same brush to pick up the perigrey; it will already have the mid-tone color on it.

Veronica's spotting palette

Drop spotting colors into wells in amounts needed for that day. With the brush, spread a small amount of dye around each well. This will evaporate to become a darker shade.

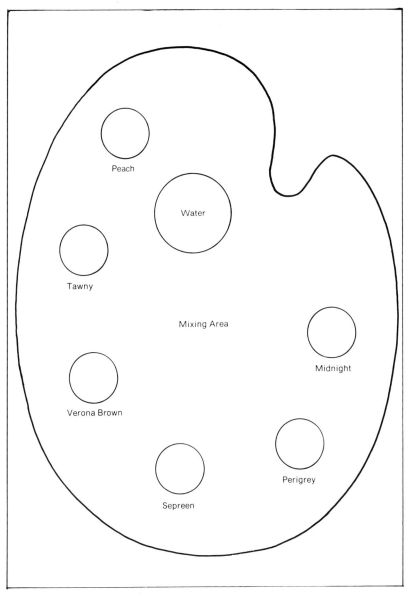

Peach

Water

Tawny

Mixing Area

Midnight

Verona Brown

Perigrey

Sepreen

Veronica's Spotting Palette

Subject needs retouching for blemishes and small scars. (Unretouched print).

Left: Blemishes retouched with VCII, blended with diluted VCII and worked up to hot spots (highlights) in certain areas. (Print retouched but not spotted.)

Right: Print spotted with tawny dye, the perfect spotting color. (Print retouched and spotted with just dyes, no spray or pencils.)

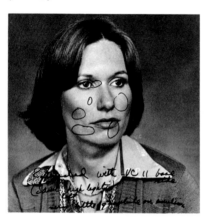

Retouching glares on glasses on prints

To correct glare on glasses, first study the print. Wide dark frames leave a very dark shadow around the glare. The narrow metal frames often leave a natural skin tone. Use a black mask to check the color around the glare, most likely finding the area very dark.

Use dyes to correct these areas. Verona brown and midnight will probably be the shades needed. It may be necessary to mix the two

100

shades. Work from the lightest shade to the darkest. Add color in layers, building to the density needed.

Steps to follow:
1. Draw in the missing eye, lid and lashes using a wet-dry brush.
2. Start with light dye and then add other colors.
3. Work from outside edge of glare to the center, if small glare. If large, get color needed or #2 brush. Move back and forth in the center, almost to the edge. Then with tip of brush, fill in unfinished lines.

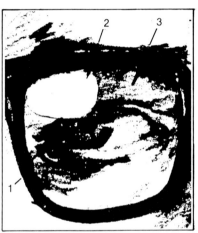

1. Draw in the missing eye, lid and lashes, remembering to use a wet dry brush.

2. Start with light dye and then add other colors.

3. Work from outside edge of glare to center.

Print Retouched Photo - Retouched with Veronica's Spotting Colors. The dye blends into the emulsion, leaving no trace. (This print has not been sprayed.)
MAN - Shine on top of head reduced. All lines reduced. Jawline, neckline and mouth softened.
WOMAN - Hair filled in by adding curl on top. Glares on glasses corrected. Age lines softened on cheeks and around mouth to make skin nicer. Neckline blended.

Red eyes in candid photographs

To remove red eye appearance in or on a print, neutralize. A light wash of cyan will return eye to normal shade. If the color still is not right, add a little of the person's natural color after the eye is neutralized.

Flexichroming — dry dye method

Kodak Retouching Colors are often referred to as flexichroming. Just about every studio and lab has a set or two of the colors, yet few people realize how important this set can be. It's a perfect dye for photography to enhance color, neutralize the wrong color out of a print and do general spotting. With one set, you can make tube dyes, a set of liquid dyes and a Kodak palette.

The supplies you will need for flexichroming are a vaporizer or a bottle warmer, cotton and tissue and a set of Kodak Retouching Colors.

How to flexichrome prints With the dry dye method, dye corrections are made by rubbing dye into the area then wiping off the excess.

Be sure to wipe out the eyes on a portrait, clean teeth, wipe down highlights on forehead, nose, cheeks and chin in correct areas. Then, check over prints for streaks of dye not correctly rubbed.

When corrected print is finished, steam lightly. A baby bottle warmer with a vaporizer cover which can be purchased at a drug store, can be used. The vaporizer cover prevents any specks of water from touching the print. Hold print approximately 12 inches above vaporizer for a few seconds. When print is competely dry (I sometimes use a hair blow-dryer), wipe print clean with dry tissue. This will remove any excess wax or finger prints. It is important to do this before spraying.

What if more work is needed on the print, such as more color or an added color? With this method of dry dye, it is possible to apply one color, steam clean a print and repeat until the results are satisfactory. All corrections must be made before spraying print. The color goes directly into the print.

When print is readied for spraying, wipe it clean, then spray. Spray lightly to seal in artwork. This method is good for enhancing backgrounds, clothing, complexions and for neutralizing unwanted color.

To remove flexichrome-set colors, use clear household ammonia. It is safe, fast and very efficient. When clean, wash a few minutes, dry thoroughly with hair dryer, and start corrections again.

Explanation of photos: Dry dye method, with Kodak Retouching Colors is a method commonly referred to as "flexichroming," which means to flex a color into the emulsion of a print.

This photograph of the policeman was corrected by the flexichrome method because the badge on the hat was too bright and his hand is far too noticeable, therefore, distracting from his face.

To correct these, the following steps were used:

1. A neutral dye corrected the badge and hand.
2. VC flesh added color to his hand and part of his face.
3. To add the shadow to his hand, use the neutral tint.

How to make dry dye tubes

To make a dry dye tube, use metal lipstick tubes. Place the tubes in the freezer, and when needed, use a sharp knife to remove the old lipstick. Then clean the tube with facial tissue; washing it is unnecessary.

In the bottom of the tube, place a small round piece of firm cardboard or paper. This is to prevent dye waste that would go through the prongs and fill the bottom.

Place the dye jar or jars in a pan, on a warm stove or in the oven, loosening covers so they can be easily lifted off when dye is melted. Melt slowly; do not cook dye.

When the dye is melted, simply use a narrow, warmed table knife, dipping it into the dye. Drip it slowly into the tube. Let dye cool and then twist the tube firmly, loosening the sides.

The final step is to label the dye tube. Put a touch of color on a small white strip and scotch-tape it to the bottom half of the tube with name of color type next to color.

Caring for tubes Refrigeration is recommended to prevent melting of dyes and for an even consistency in blending. Test colors on developed white paper or an unwanted photograph to make sure colors do not streak and that they blend evenly. To avoid breakage, swivel up about a quarter inch.

Making a set of Kodak liquid dyes

After making your set of tubes, some dye will be left over. Take a small amount (about the size of a pea) and put it into a one ounce bottle with an eye dropper, which can be purchased at a drug store. Add distilled or tap water (it depends on your type of water). Let it stand overnight, then shake well the next day. The liquid dye is ready. Make a bottle of each color for a complete set.

I use liquid dye when making a Kodak palette. Place a couple of drops of each color on palettes as instructed or use plexiglass. It will be a real time saver. Place palette inside an envelope when not in use so that it will not pick up dust.

A Kodak palette is used for wet neutralizing small areas, such as unwanted green from prints that have been over dyed or to neutralize out of other colors. It can also be used for commercial prints that often have vivid colors, not subtle like those found in portrait photography.

It's a good idea to have Kodak Form E-70 to use for neutralizing. I always keep one of these charts in my work area; it helps prevent mistakes.

Kodak from E-70

To control or neutralize an off-color area — use chart below to guide you.

```
RED........................................... CYAN
GREEN.................................... MAGENTA
BLUE........................................ ORANGE
*PURPLE.................................... YELLOW
```
*Purple is a mixture of blue and magenta.
Note that this chart is applicable to both negatives and prints.

Scatches caused from emulsion side   If the scratch is red, add Cyan and dilute color. If the scratch is yellow, add magenta and then cyan. Be sure to dilute each time. This method is applicable strictly to prints.

Lumo Color pencils

The Lumo Color pencil is a Geman product that looks like a wax pencil but works like a flexichrome dry dye. Be sure you first sharpen the pencils by wiping sideways on white work paper.

Use your pencils as follows:

1. To enhance a color, use desired color pencil, applying to the print like a crayon.
2. Take a piece of cotton, blend color around and rub into emulsion.
3. Wipe off excess penciling.
4. If color has been overlapped, use the white pencil to remove unwanted color or wet cotton swab.
5. If you are dissatisfied with color, take a swab of wet cotton and wipe all the color off; let dry and repeat steps 1-3.
6. When print is finished, spray lightly to seal in art work. I generally spray very lightly a couple of times and then give it a final spray. Steaming can also be done.

Although this set of pencils isn't really designed for photographs, they are effective for working on small areas. Following are a few hints for color combinations:

1. For flesh, use brown and red at the same time and blend, being careful not to use too much red.
2. For sky, use blue and white and blend. Blue alone is too strong.
3. For trees, use green in shadows, a touch of brown here and there, and a touch of yellow in highlight areas.
4. The black will help in areas needing added density.
5. The red is almost a carmine and can be used for enhancing the lips or cheeks of a small photograph.
6. Brown is good for adding color to hair, blond or light brown. It's also good for hairs that pick up highlight around the head. Use pencil and blend in with your finger.

Lumo Color pencil colors are excellent mediums for candids. They add to missing colors due to fabrics, as well as dress up where light is too bright.

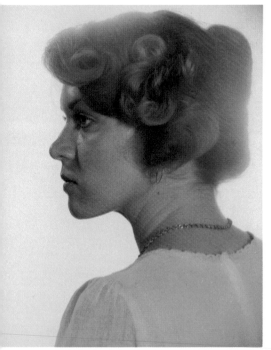 

PROBLEM: Photographer wants more color in hair. This is a display print.

Correction quickly accomplished with Lumo color. Lumo brown is just right for dark blonds.

Opaquing a print

Opaque can be applied directly to prints on the emulsion side or on a sprayed print. It is not transparent; it covers completely and blocks out the light.

Because opaques hide and cover, they are used for fixing teeth, opening eyes, covering black specks, removing the wrong highlight from the eyes and putting in the correct one. They can also be used to mend dresses and fill in small obscure objects in the background.

The supplies needed to opaque are a Grumbacher's Gamma Photo Retouch Kit (25-14) or Designer's Gouache, Grumbacher's brush — #178-000 (for fine detail) and clear acetate.

No matter what type of correction, the right tone or shade of opaque can be found by using clear acetate first over the area, determining if it need be lighter or darker or of the warmer or cooler colors. By working on acetate, the right correction can be achieved.

To apply opaque, use the sable brush suggested. This brush must be wet to be able to pick up the opaque, and the opaque must be applied immediately before it dries on the brush.

Practice a few strokes on an extra print or the acetate getting the feel of the right opaque consistency. If the brush is too wet, it will not pick up enough opaque and the correction will not be covered. On the other hand, if too much opaque is picked up, the ridges will be left on the print. Consistent results will be achieved by time and practice.

When using opaque, do not try to wipe it with a finger or skewer. This will only make it messy. Keep the brush supple for easy control by touching here and there.

When making a correction on a print or adding teeth, place clear acetate over the problem area and do the art work to see if it is the correct color and/or if the art work is as it should be. Let dry. When it appears to be correct, apply opaque directly on the print. When sprayed, the opaque will darken. Therefore, always opaque slightly lighter.

To remove small spots, wet a toothpick skewer and touch spot to dampen and loosen. Turn skewer to clean side and lift off the opaque. If the large area is wrong, wash print about ten minutes and check to see if color stains are present. If they are, put ammonia in water a few minutes, rinse well, dry with hair dryer and try again.

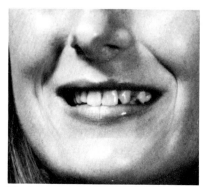
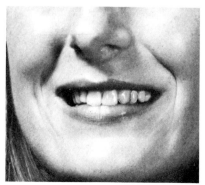

Missing tooth to be corrected with opaque.
To judge correct color, put mask over teeth. Use clear acetate to determine

proper shade of opaque, practicing on the acetate before applying to print.
Spray and highlight with prisma pencil.

How to spray the print

1. When emulsion corrections (dyes, flexichroming, spotting) have been made, wipe the print off completely with facial tissue or clean cotton. Sprays will cover much better when the print is clean.
2. Whether using a spray gun or spray can, remember the nozzle must be clean. Soak the gun nozzle in thinners at the end of each day. The spray can is cleaned by turning it upside-down, releasing spray to clear stem.
3. When applying from a can, prepare the spray by holding can at the top. Swing the can back and forth in a pendulum manner so that the ball in the can will roll around and crush the matte. DO NOT SHAKE UP AND DOWN VIGOROUSLY. Too much shaking will cause the ball to go up and down making the matte chunky. It will also cause the combustion in the can to form bubbles, making it spit out specks of lacquer and white particles. Be sure to swing long enough to prevent those white specks.
4. Spray the print from the bottom upward, holding the gun or spray can about 12 inches from the print. This distance will insure an even spray. Holding a can too far away creates a fine dust as the spray dries before it hits the print. If this should happen, move in closer and re-spray to melt the first spray.

If you are using lacquer with a tooth for pencil work, spray the entire print for an even matte coating and then wet spray the work area. Make sure the work area is completely covered by holding print to the light. If no sparkly effect appears and it looks wet, then it is sprayed correctly for pencil corrections.

5. Let print dry flat to prevent dripping, allow it to dry thoroughly.

6. When print is ready for pencil correction, be sure the Prisma pencil is very sharp. Sharpen at ends with no number. Even if pencils have been freshly sharpened, point the pencil on the work paper. The finer the point; the finer the retouching. Use colors a shade lighter than is called for as they will turn darker when sprayed. Check out the color first by using a black mask and then by testing color on white paper. Apply Prisma pencils lightly as though retouching a negative. Blend lightly and in layers. Using this method, two or three colors can be on one coat of spray. It looks grainy only when the leads have been pressed too hard and large strokes have been made or spray is not on smoothly. If wrong color has been used, erase lightly with kneader eraser. It will remove the pencil and leave the spray workable.

7. When print is completed, apply final re-spray carefully. Protect the art work. Spray lightly once, twice and then a third time. The art work is now sealed and will not melt. All too often this is done incorrectly. Spray final coat lightly. Matte special is a nice profes-

sional finish to be applied here, or a lustre finish. In humid areas, moisture should not be allowed to gather on print. Spray the print gradually; do not flood. This prevents the print from turning white or light cyan.

Retouching with sprays and oils

Sprays and oils are used in retouching in many ways, enhancing prints (backgrounds, hair, facial corrections), restoring color prints and as a final step in airbrushing. The necessary supplies are: McDonald sprays or other quality brands, Marshall's or Grumbacher's or Winsor & Newton's Oil Colors, brushes (size depends on print and type of work to be done).

Enhancing prints

To add color with oils you must first spray the print very well. Luster spray is used for a light shade of oil color, and matte special spray can be used, though the oil color will appear as a darker shade.

Spraying will seal the print for good results. Hold the print at an angle so that light will shine directly on it. If, after being sprayed, the print has an even finish, then the print is ready for oil. Shiny speckles, however, means that the print has not been sprayed enough. Continue spraying until the finish is even.

When the print is ready, apply a light coat of linseed oil and wipe down very well, assuring a smooth base for the oil color. Add desired color. If more is desired or needed, this method can be repeated by applying several coats of spray, oil color — be sure to hair dry spray each time.

For color restoration

This method is used to revive colors in faded natural color prints. Apply to flesh, clothing and backgrounds. There are times when a print turns blue or green in areas. To correct this, mix oil color to the proper shade and paint it over the discoloration. Sometimes it will be necessary to go over the entire print with an oil tint or heavy oil. If the face is involved, coat the entire face to create an even, over-all color. This will insure against uneven fading.

Spray and oils can be used to restore damaged prints. For example, if a negative is torn or badly scratched in an area showing a group of people or fine details and cannot be airbrushed, oil is best for the correction. Use a fine sable brush, perhaps a Winsor & Newton Series 2, #1 for fine details and a #52 flat for clothing and props. This method removes heavy scratches or cracks and helps put in arms or trees.

There are times when dye spotting and dye corrections can begin correcting a print and then oils added. This keeps the print more natural.

Oil corrections and airbrushing

Airbrushing leaves a dull finish even with sprays — especially on a plain area or background. To add a sheen or gloss, airbrush the area, spray print with Lustre and then apply a coat of oil, similar to the color on background. This greatly improves the print, especially if you are correcting a natural color print or adding a color background.

Print retouching with sprays and Prisma pencils or perwent

Some sprays have a very hard protective finish and never scratch, but others can scratch easily. They also offer many professional finishes from matte retouch and matte special to a lustre or clear. There are many

Spray and pencils can be used to neutralize an unwanted color out, cover mistakes and print retouch environmental photographs that are too small to negative retouch.

brands and like any product, there are superior and inferior finishes. Using them in the proper manner is important for effective art work.

Spray and pencils can be used to neutralize an unwanted color out in small areas, cover mistakes and print retouch environmental photographics that are too small to negative retouch.

There are a few myths about sprays which need to be cleared up. Very often the user causes problems by improper usage. Shaking the spray can the wrong way, or applying spray incorrectly, or the problem could simply be the print itself. Understanding the problems and becoming more knowledgeable of spray will insure a better print. Some specific problems are tar spots, magenta spots, white dust, white specks and spitting laquer spots.

Often problems can arise after spraying. Discoloration spots are caused from improper washing. Proper washing is very important in the darkroom or in a processor. As mentioned above, tar spots are a problem. These are not caused by the sprays. They are on the paper. The spray just brings them out. It is a problem of improper mixing of chemicals and the wrong temperature.

Applying acrylics to photography

Acrylics can be used to retouch prints. They adhere directly on the emulsion, match colors and allow for an instant master background. They can be used for changing backgrounds, color restorations, making a portrait from a snapshot and for quick art corrections.

The trick to working with acrylics is knowing how to apply them. The supplies needed are a #1 or #2 outline brush (not expensive), a half-inch or a quarter-inch bristle or acrylic brush, water, paper towel and basic acrylics. The palette should be paper disposable. For disposable pallettes, use old or rejected color prints, whose back is perfect for this use. Cut old prints into 4×5's.

What colors are recommended? Simply look at the clothing and background. Suggested colors are: Hooker's green, Payne's gray, burnt umber and titanium white.

Method for applying acrylics for background or making portrait from group photograph.
   1. Mount print.
   2. Put acrylics on disposable palette.

3. Arrange color on palette, picking up color without over-blending. Make a wash of acrylics by adding a small amount of water, painting a thin coat around the subject. This will protect the shape of the head and avoid making a ridge of paint. Apply with a soft brush, about a #1 or #2. Here again, the size of the brush will be dependent on the size of the print. Use color that will be used to brush stroke.
4. Blend on the background itself. Use acrylic brush (according to the size of the print) and use a basket weave stroke.

This way   That Way   Tie Together

Blending on the background, using a basket weave stroke.

5. Use two colors for background and white and a ½" or 2" brush. Payne's gray or burnt umber can be used as a base color with a little white to complement, yet not detract from, the subject. Sometimes a third color is used in the top corners to bring out the hair or clothing.
6. Work fast to avoid drying. Do not over-blend. Always keep in mind to make the subject look better and make the background less obvious.
7. If the acrylic doesn't adhere in spots, let the spots dry and go back to them later. This results from the emulsion becoming too wet from an overwet brush.
8. Work from "wash" outline to the edge of the print. Keep colors similar. To keep the brush workable, dip the tip in water.
9. When finished, let the print dry thoroughly. A hair dryer can be used to speed this process.
10. Spray print with a retouch lacquer with a tooth and use Prisma pencils to tie the subject to the background. Use matching pencils for the hair line, retouch blemishes, soften circles under the eyes, clothing and for any extra retouching on the print. This will soften the edge between the subject and background, placing subject in front.

11. Re-spray lightly, using matte special or lustre to seal in pencil work and insuring that art work will not become wet and run.
12. Apply Pro-Texture Plus to subject and make the strokes look like a painting. Follow the outline in small strokes. Be sure to blend the subject and background together. Avoid a sharp edge.
13. Let dry thoroughly. Spray again with matte special for the final finish as the Pro-Texture Plus will leave a shiny finish. Matte special will tone it down to satisfaction.

Before applying acrylics.

A thin, flat coat of acrylic has been applied around subject's body.

Completed photograph. A portrait is made from a group shot.

Brush application of Pro-Texture Plus Pro-Texture Plus is a new, water-based texturing medium. Because it holds the brush strokes much better than the Standard Pro-Texture, it is recommended for all brush texturing. Don't confuse its appearance with the other gels on the market. McDonald's Pro-Texture Plus is an adherent that drys completely transparent without yellowing.

Steps to apply Pro-Texture Plus
1. Spray print with wet coat of McDonald's Pro-Tecta-Cote Matte or matte special lacquer. The print must be sealed before applying Pro-Texture Plus.
2. Apply Pro-Texture Plus directly from container with a slant-cut brush, following the contour of the subject. The material will retain the bristle marks without reworking.
3. Allow to dry thoroughly until hard. The white will disappear, leaving a glossy, transparent finish.
4. Spray two medium coats of McDonald Pro-Tecta-Cote Lustre or matte special, as desired.

Note: Brushes can be directly cleaned after use by rinsing in hot water.

Airbrush

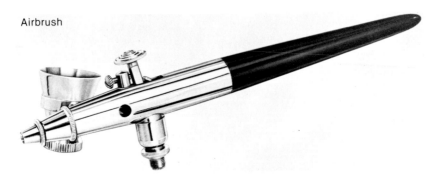

Airbrush Segments

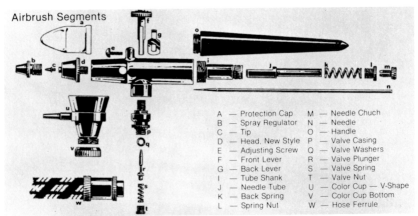

A	— Protection Cap	M	— Needle Chuch
B	— Spray Regulator	N	— Needle
C	— Tip	O	— Handle
D	— Head, New Style	P	— Valve Casing
E	— Adjusting Screw	Q	— Valve Washers
F	— Front Lever	R	— Valve Plunger
G	— Back Lever	S	— Valve Spring
I	— Tube Shank	T	— Valve Nut
J	— Needle Tube	U	— Color Cup — V-Shape
K	— Back Spring	V	— Color Cup Bottom
L	— Spring Nut	W	— Hose Ferrule

The Air Gauge
and Regulator

The Air Line
Filter

The Compressor

116

CHAPTER THIRTEEN

Airbrushing

The airbrush is a device for spraying inks, dyes and paints powered by compressed air. There are many types of airbrushes available for different types of work. Some designed for detail work are so fine that a skilled operator can spray a line like a pencil mark. There are used in both mechanical and decorative drawing, often with stencils to confine the spray to certain areas.

Airbrushes are also used for photo retouching. I use the Thayer & Chandler model (pictured) for color prints and restoration.

The other necessary materials are a compressor (or tank), hose (different sizes), air gauge and regulator, trap or airline filter, paints, opaques, brushes, palette, plastic bottles, friskets, acetate, paper punch and scissors or Exacto knife.

How to use an airbrush

Make sure to clean all finger prints off the print before beginning airbrushing. Set the pressure of the compressor between 25 to 30 pounds. Attach the airbrush to hose connection. Put color cup on the airbrush firmly by using a screwing motion to hold in place.

Get to know the airbrush by practicing with it. Learn how to adjust lines and how to regulate the quality of the spray. Learn to blend, to make narrow wide lines, circles, pyramids and cylinders.

To hold the brush correctly:

1. Place forefinger on the finger lever — at the first knuckle, not the tip of the finger. Hold the brush as a pen.
2. Press down slowly. This will cause the air to release.
3. Pull back slowly to release paint. To increase the flow pull lever all the way back, still keeping a downward pressure.
4. To make a narrow line, hold brush near the board. To control the line, turn the adjusting screw which is located near front lever (finger level). Balance hand with small finger against the print.
5. To make a wider line, move the brush back about six to eight inches, controlling the line width by pulling the brush further away from the work.
6. When finished, do not let lever fly forward. Release lever slowly, to avoid spitting spots.
7. When finished with airbrush, clean at once. Most problems arise from brushes not being cleaned thoroughly.
8. Put clean water in color cup and blow through a few times. Pull needle and wipe off. Now put finger on spray regulator and blow water through back into color cup. Repeat several times. Then unscrew connection nipple and insert into the color cup and pull back finger lever. This will allow air to blow through the airbrush and will dry the inside.

   For those living in southern areas where it is humid, keep the needle packed separately from the brush to avoid rusting.

Next learn the colors. Know what to buy. Improper products will mean nothing but headaches. Many art stores today do not have qualified help and often do not know or understand specific problems or needs. Request exactly what is necessary. It's always safe to buy a quality brand such as Designer's Gouache, distributed by Winsor & Newton and M. Grumbacher. This is a very fine opaque.

For mixing color, Grumbacher has a very fine book with a color chart and wheel, "Color Compass." Keep on hand a variety of mixed colors. There are one or two ounce plastic bottles available. These can be used when preparing Designer's Gouache for use.

Fill the bottle half full with water. Add three-quarters of a tube of color. Shake the bottle well. Two or three different colors can be added to achieve a certain shade. If mixture becomes too thick, add water.

Some suggestions
1. Use lamp black to tone down vivid color.
2. Use black and orange for flesh. You can vary the shade according to the amount of orange used.
3. Black and yellow in various amounts can make a suitable green. You can change shades.

When using opaques, remember they are very light when wet. They will darken when dry and become even darker when sprayed. Learn to mix a color and test it. If it's necessary to match a wall or dress or suit, use the color chart and match as closely as possible.

Practice on sheets of white paper. Easels allow airbrushing to be done in a standing position. It is often much easier to stand than sit and often will afford more control. Butcher paper (white) which is strong, inexpensive and used in all art work is good for practicing. Cover the easel and practice.
A. Learn how to control the brush.
B. Learn how to hold the brush at different angles.
C. Learn to make angles and circles and put shadows around.

Practice, practice and practice. Make lines, dots and tubes.

Hold airbrush in this manner. Start on subject and spray to outer edge.

To check the color consistency, hold a clear acetate over the area that has to be matched. If the shade looks right, apply alcohol to a piece of acetate to see if color will darken to right shade.

After doing this a few times, you will learn to know the shading of opaques. Sometimes in making a correction on a large area such as a wall, it is easier to airbrush the entire wall than to try to match the small area.

Another medium for airbrushing is liquid color. It is a way of adding a transparent color to an area to enhance a color, to change a color, or to neutralize a color. (See page with neutralizing chart.) Practice. Dilute transparent colors enough to get the shade needed. It is better to add layers of color gradually, than to add too much color at one time. Liquid color can be used to add blue to skies, green to grass and trees and color to water.

The DON'T'S in airbrushing

1. Don't use hot water for cleaning airbrush.
2. Don't take the airbrush apart at first trouble. See if the air pressure is right; try running clean water through; see if spray regulator is adjusted right; see if needle is set for the line wanted.
3. Don't bend the point of the needle.
4. Don't insert anything in spray regulator when it is on the airbrush.
5. Don't enlarge opening in spray regulator.
6. Don't use the reamer except in extreme cases, and do not press too hard when turning it.
7. Don't insert anything in the tip, or pinch or batter it in any way.
8. Don't let your colors be exposed to dirt and lint.
9. Don't use any colors that are not finely ground.
10. Don't let others handle your brush. Loan it as little as possible.
11. Don't fail to keep spray regulator free from dried color.
12. Don't spoil thread on spray regulator by starting it wrong and then forcing it.
13. Don't snap front lever.

To airbrush, make mask; make two prints; cut out subject on one print and use a paper punch to make little holes on subject about ¼ inch on inside of outline. Apply cut-out directly over the other work print.

Photo of before and after:

1. full print
2. mask
3. finished print
   a. tied outline to subject in few missed areas with 178 Grumbacher brush.
   b. sprayed print with retouch spray.
   c. made art corrections and again put subjects in front with (brought subject out with) Prisma pencils.
   d. stroke on outline to soften hard line.
   e. sprayed again slowly and several times to protect art work — use a Matte Special or Lustre.

121

Put little pieces of masking tape over the holes to hold subject in place preventing a sharp edge around the subject when airbrushing. The air from the brush lifts the edge of the subject just enough to avoid build up.

A mask can also be made of clear acetate by placing it over the subject. Trace subject with marking pen and cut out acetate. Punch holes as noted above. Art work can be done with opaques and brush in black and white or color. Added artwork is often needed when working on commercial prints, use same gouache.

Remove mask, lift carefully being careful to keep mask near work print. Where there needs a bit more opaque to tie the background to subject, take your #178 opaque brush and pick up opaque from mask. If chin needs to be fixed, pick up paint from the edge of chin area. This insures that color will match.

When finished, spray with retouch spray very lightly several times. When dry, use Prima pencils to touch up here and there. Touch up hairline — match color to correct areas. You may have to touch the background here and there, too, on spit spots. Also facial corrections may have to be made. Be sure to use a shade lighter. Re-spray with matte special, very slowly, perhaps going over the matte special to obtain a nice sheen. Use oil lightly; rub down; spray again with matte special.

CHAPTER FOURTEEN

Restoration

My aim in restoration of prints is to restore the photographs as closely as possible to the original prints. To do so, the negative and the print work require dyes, graphite and an etching knife.

When receiving a request from a customer about an old photograph for restoration, study the print to judge how much work has to be done. After evaluating, give a price estimate. Explain that this type of art work is time-comsuming and that they will be notified when it is finished. Have them sign the order sheet.

Ask the customer's approval to spot out the white lines or clean the print so that more details can be seen. To spot the print, use a Verona brown dye and fill in the white scratches. Be sure to dilute the dye and test a small area before doing this to make sure it matches. Also clean a small patch on the print with trichloroethylene or something similar to see if it will clean, but do this only with the customer's permission. If trichloroethylene cannot be obtained at a drugstore, go to the local dry cleaners and purchase some of their cleaning fluid or to a druggist for something similar.

After spotting and cleaning print, copy it with 4×5 film (Kodak copy film). Retouch the negative. Make two prints if airbrushing is required. If not, make one 8×10 or 11×14 print. Do the artwork on the print. A larger size allows more detailed work for second copy negative. When reduced art work will look better.

When preparing to oil color, make prints on "G" or "R" Ektalure paper for good color work. For browntone, I suggest silenium. Before adding oil color, accentuate the faded areas with diluted Verona brown dye. Adding color to a restored print the way the photographers used to do is called tinting. It is done by using very little color.

Directions for Application of Oils:

1. Apply basic flesh with skewer over face. Marshall's oils can be used for this. Do subject first and then paint background. (Arrange basic colors — a very small amount of flesh on palette (disposable if for only one or two prints). Basic colors can be Verona brown, flesh, blue or green, cheek, lip and color for clothing. Usually all of the colors will be in the Marshall's Oil Hobbyset.

   Flesh colors: 1. Women — flesh
   2. Men — Flesh 2

2. Wipe down all over.

3. Wipe out highlights to give roundness.

4. For cheek, use little in the area you apply. Cheek paint is a strong color, use very little. It is easier to apply if you mix flesh with cheek.

5. For lips, mix with flesh. Women: add a little flesh to lip color. Men: half and half.

6. For eyes, clean first with kneaded eraser and then use either Prisma pencil or toothpick skewer. Very little color is needed. If using skewer, pick up a small amount of color and then wipe excess off to make sure you don't overdo eyes.

7. Apply color of hair, wipe down after applying correct color.

Restoration background

Backgrounds for oil paintings   After the subject has been tinted, use the paints which have been left on the palette. Mix them into a subtle color. The grey greens, grey blues, or Verona brown can also be used.

When restoring old portrait photographs, sometimes the background is badly marred. A nice background can be painted by using the left-over paints on your palette. When portraits are in this poor condition, it is best to advise the customer to order small sizes. The 5×7 and miniatures are always nice with a brush oil background.

Use the oil brush (Series 52, No.3, Winsor & Newton) to mix in a little titanium white with the brown. This is a good basic color which can be lighter or darker, depending on what is desired for the background. It will appear muddy. Using a small amount of the blue left over from the eyes and the flesh as a bright color, color can be added to the basic color by working the added colors into the corners of the photograph, picking up the brown as blending.

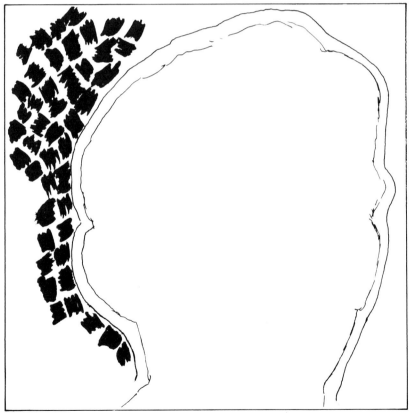

Start in this area using the basic color; add color. The strokes should be small and not over-blended.

Leave narrow space around subject. When finished, wipe brush on facial tissue until dry and feather background to subject. This way, a heavy line can be avoided.

Spray print when dry. Matte special is a suggested finish.

Print was copied by horizontal copy camera — Burke & James Princeton, lens — Goerz "Red Dot" Artar, lighting — 2 flood lights, 500 watts, tungston, film — professional copy film by Kodak. Results: a good image.

Retouching was needed and accomplished with "dark" dye and HB graphite. When printed, image appeared better, but more work was needed.

Print was spotted with Verona Brown. This dye blends perfectly with browntone prints - great for restoration.

When photo was finished and dried, it was sprayed with matte special. Then it was copied again, in case customer ordered another photo, which they did, ordering 3 oils also. This is the second copy.

Before and After. Subject needed both eyelids raised.

Making art corrections to open eyes

One thing which must be kept in mind, when opening eyes, be sure they are looking in the same direction. Working with the basic dye, hold print at a distance to see if it is in the proper perspective. Also cover one eye to see if opened eye is opened enough. Sometimes it may look just right but by checking the suggested way the facts are more obvious.

To open small eyes as on candids and groups, you need only use basic dye and a touch of opaque. If print is sprayed, use retouch spray and Prisma pencils.

How to open eyes

1. First determine where eyes are looking, where the light source is coming from and then work with half-closed eye or less. I use dye as a base to achieve the natural look.

2. Lift pupil to desired size with your darkest dye or brown mixed in.

3. Add raised eyelid with brown dye. Shape like other lid on opened eye. Eyelashes can also be added at this time, keep them natural. Lashes are not even.

4. Opaque old lid out with grey. Use black **mask** to check other eye by placing over the whites of the eyes. Whites **are** not really white but grey. When using opaque, remember it will turn darker when sprayed and keep on the light side. At this time, also add highlight, apply to side from which light comes, either 11:00 or 1:00, using light grey.

5. Spray print with retouch spray.

6. Do final art work with Prisma art pencils. Touch up pupil. Add color to the iris. This is done by making fine strokes to look like flecks. Only do this to half of the eye. Keep it natural. Strengthen lines around iris and lids. Sometimes a touch of pencil here and there can make a tremendous difference in corrections.

7. Spray again very lightly to seal in art work and then spray to give a final professional touch.

CHAPTER FIFTEEN

Finishing the print

Finishing photographs, making them artistically correct and ready for packaging, adds a final touch of professionalism. Spraying the prints, selecting mounts, folders, framing and even the wrap or box selected for the final presentation of a completed order are part of the finishing process.

Finishing encompasses a variety of elegant touches. It will be dependent on the price charged, on what the customer likes and where you set your level of prestigue and value.

Spraying a print

Start with spraying the final print. There are several sprays available including matte, which is very flat and dull, which subdues the color considerably. Matte special is a semi-gloss, excellent for a professional finish. It is neither too shiny or too dull, just right. Lustre is more of a satin finish, and clear is very shiny. Clear is a good choice for commercial prints.

Mounting and displaying prints

The importance of display or presentation can never be stressed enough. Mounting a print is an added protection from cracking or creasing. Mounting boards are available in double and single weight. The weight selected may depend on how the product is to be sold. For example, in preparing a print to be framed and the print is not a package deal, but in the high-priced presentation, then use a quality, double-weight board. If, on the other hand, it's a school contract with little profit margin, then use the single-weight board.

Yet another type for promotional purposes is canvas board. It is reasonably priced and really adds quality to a print.

Canvassing

Canvassing a print is indeed an art in itself. Learning to strip a print and canvas it will provide added satisfaction. McDonald Products has developed a method than can be done easily.

Preparation for canvassing is as follows:

Have a mounting press accessible. This is used for both mounting prints on mounting boards and canvas. The linen texture canvas used for photographs, lamin-all, brush or spray gun, frames and pliers are also needed.

To canvas a print, strip the emulsion from the back and paper back. This is done by starting the edge with a sharp knife, such as an Exacto knife. Pull print loose enough to be able to put end of print on a rod and roll the rest of print off, or strip in sections.

Then place emulsion face down on a cardboard and clip to board with large loose wire pins (or can be made of clothes hangers). Be sure print is flat. Board should be slightly smaller to prevent curling. Apply lamin-all to entire print. Let stand until tacky. Be sure to cover area completely. This can be done with a brush or spray gun.

Take cardboard and print and apply to canvas, making sure print is in line with linen of canvas. Also make sure there are no flaws such as knots. Press print slightly on canvas. Remove board, then take print and canvas and place on Teflon neoprene pad, positioning print face down on pad. Cover with cloth or sheet of Teflon to keep press clean. Hold print and canvas and carefully slide into press.

If print does not have a good canvas texture, because lamin-all was too dry, moisten emulsion and press again. Press about 45 seconds at about 210°F.

Then remove print from press. Either put on a stretcher frame or mount on masonite. When stretching on frames, use method used by artists. Start in center of frame, staple a few (about 3) and pull tightly to opposite side, using pliers. Staple about three more staples and then turn to other end of frame. Staple a few in the middle and again to opposite side.

Now start in first area and staple a few more on each side, repeating this method of stapling gradually, working around the frame. When at corners, trim and fold corners. Make sure there is no heavy fold to interfere with framing. Stretching a canvas in this manner prevents wrinkles and uneveness.

To add a final finish to canvas, use sprays, brush texturing, antiquing and florentining. I suggest the booklet, "The McDonald Method of Print Finishing" to obtain suggestions and further information.

To assure longevity of your canvas mounted print, the following is recommended:

1. Maintain 30-50% relative humidity year round. Less than this may cause frames to separate, and the print to crack and/or pull away from canvas. Excess moisture can cause sagging in the canvas and the print to appear "rippled." Though the canvas may stretch or shrink from too little or too much moisture, the print will remain the same size.
2. Allow print to "adjust" 10 to 14 days in home or studio. Rippled canvases are often temporary and will within this short time correct themselves. Avoid placing a canvas mounted print above any heating or cooling registers.
3. Don't try to cover print. Trapping moisture in will only harm the canvas.
4. Keep print clean. Use mild not abrasive chemicals, cleaners or instruments, applying ever so gently.

Framing

Framing is also an important part of finishing and can become a very lucrative business as well. Beautiful, quality framing is more than just necessity for the photograph. It should also be considered as important as other furnishings in one's home. Today there are many beautiful selections to suit almost any photograph — modern and restored.

The frame should never distract from the subject in the photograph, but should enhance or attract to the subject. A frame should be selected or suggested to the customer when the portrait is completed. Consideration should be given also to the person's home decor and a frame selected to blend with the decor.

When using matts or matting, select colors that complement the photograph. A variety of color choices are available. Try a print in a matte before putting the order together. Also, check for good color balance. Don't overdo it when matting portraits and photographs. DO NOT use too bright a matte or it will overpower the subject or the photograph's story.

A resourceful photographer will select both matte and frame before the customer sees the final product. This ensures the right frame for the photograph.

There will be times when a frame doesn't quite have the needed touch of color to complement the photograph. This can be easily remedied making a wash with acrylics, wiping on the frame with brush and then wiping down the wood with a cloth, leaving just a touch of color to complement the frame.

PART 4

Exercises and health tips for retouchers

CHAPTER SIXTEEN

Health tips for retouchers

Safeguarding your eyes

Although retouching itself will not hurt your eyes, improper care or neglect will. If you are approaching the forties, go to the doctor, explaining that you are a retoucher and the type of work you handle. Bring a negative and an 8×10 before and after print, showing what retouching is. Tell the doctor how many of each you do per day.

You may find you may need glasses. Having the right amount of light in your retouching machine is a great help also, so is having a properly lit room in which to work. Retouchers often develop astigmatisms. The check for this is to do retouching in the normal manner. When you finish and it looks right, turn your negative cage half-way around. If graphite marks show, then there is a chance you may have this problem. Checking for these problems before they become serious is advisable.

Young eyes often need glasses just to relax the eyes during retouching time.

Recommended exercises for retouchers

1. Drop head forward. Relax arms at your side. Roll head to both sides gently. Put chin on the chest and move it from shoulder to shoulder. Then lean head back and roll it around slowly. You will most likely hear a crackle. It's just the loosening of the tightened neck.

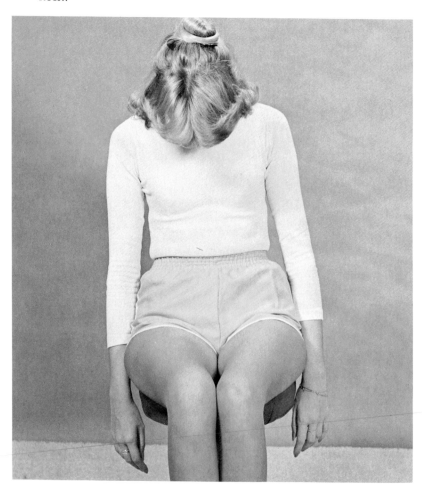

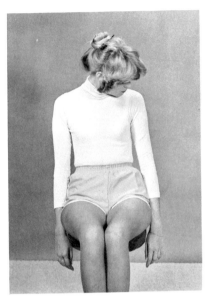

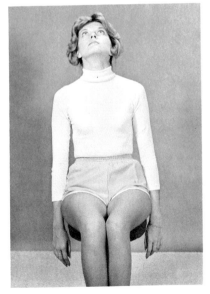
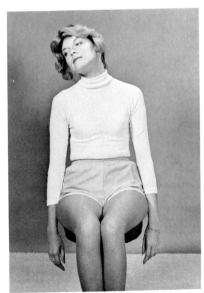

2. Lift arms straight out from sides and level with shoulders. Move and wiggle fingers. Make fists over and over again with thumb in and out. Be sure to hold arms out firm and straight.

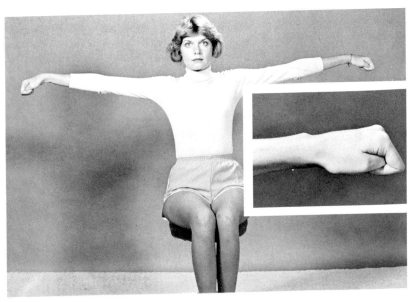

3. Stand up straight with chest out. Pull elbows back as far as possible, until you can feel the muscles of the shoulders pull. Reach forward as far as possible and pull back again.

4. While standing, turn toes in and slowly bend down without force. Hang loose, let arms limber up. It's not necessary to touch the floor. The point here is to feel the tingle in the back from neck down to heels.

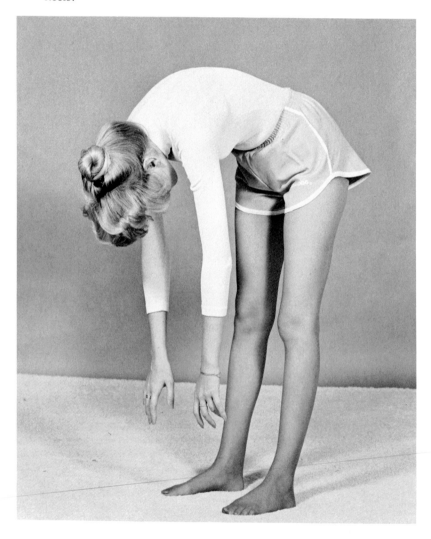

5. To exercise legs, lay down flat on back. Pull one knee up four or five times as high as possible and then repeat with the other leg.

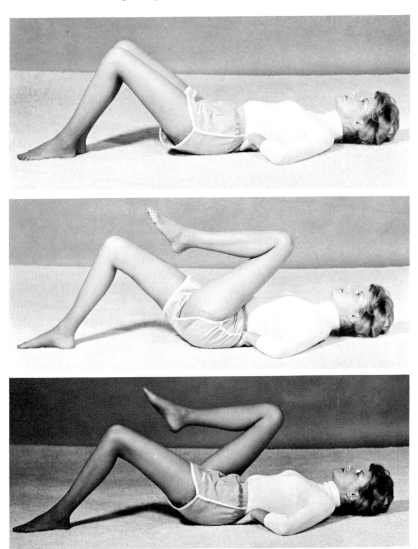

6. For backaches, lay down on the back on the floor. Put hands under body below waist so that the spine will rest comfortably. Now pull knees up, keeping feet flat on the floor. Lift one leg as high as possible four to six times, then the other leg. Then, with leg bent, pull knee back as far as possible. Do this four times. Finally, still supporting the back, lift both legs as far back as possible.

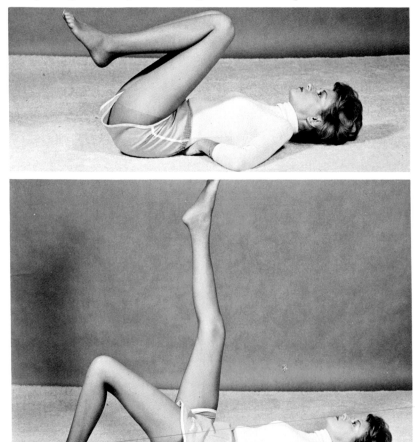

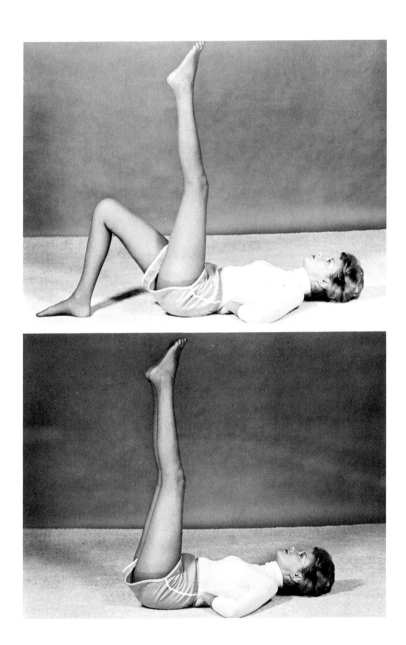

In doing these exercises, care should be taken not to overstrain. Start exercising slowly. Exercises should relax, not tire. Get in the habit of doing exercises on a regular basis — it will definitely be beneficial.

Exercising for good health

Exercise is important to the comfort of the retoucher. During the rush season, when you have to sit still longer than usual, tension will build up in the neck and shoulders. Since you will not be moving around much, circulation will suffer. Doing normal exercises the first thing in the morning can ease these tensions. Or while you are retouching and become tense, relax by sitting in a chair first, then do other exercises standing.

Sitting properly in a comfortable chair, placed at the right height for the stand, is important to the back. Sit straight to prevent the spine from slipping into the wrong position. If the table is too low or too high, tiredness will result.

When sitting at a table, place the elbow in front of the stand, positioning the arm so that just the fingers are working. Allow about four to six inches between the retouching machine and edge of the table. I recommend using two 4×5 pieces of carpeting with foam rubber backing to cushion and prevent aching elbows.

An important factor in comfort is the circulation ofthe body. Poor circulation can cause legs to swell and feet to puff up and get hot. It can even cause stomach trouble.Common sense and a doctor's advice can help. I find loose garments help as they do not cut into my wrist or legs and I definitely recommend loose clothing. Also, I keep a small foot stand or pillow under the desk or table to rest my feet occasionally. This, too, is good for circulation.

Glossary

Acetate — Moisture-proof celluloid. Variety of uses in photographic art-work.

Airbrush — Device for spraying inks, dyes and paints, powdered by compressed air.

Base — Base is the bottom, sup-port or foundation on which something rests.

Cool Color — Blue

Density — Darkness

Designer's Gouache — A selected group of colors for a very fine opaque.

Dope/Doping — A term commonly used when applying retouching fluid.

Emulsion — Coating on the base to form the photography.

Friskit Paper — A transparent paper to be applied on a drawing surface. Cut with a knife, removing unwanted outline. Used in air-brushing for commercial use.

Misket — A liquid frisket, easy to apply. Paint on; let dry. Used in art-work or airbrushing for photo masking. When finished with art-work, rub off with fingers.

Neutralize — To change unwanted colors. To gray/neutral.

Opaque — To cover. To hide.

Preview — Photographer's presen-tation of selected poses to customer.

Proof — Preview of photograph for artist to use as a study reference.

Titanium — Strongest white pig-ment available. The most opaque; and therefore less is required to ligten colors. Not affected by nor-mal atmospheric conditions.

Warm Color — Red and yellow.